Publishing Children's Poetry For 19 Years

Giving verse a voice

North Yorkshire & The North
Edited by Vivien Linton & Angela Fairbrace

First published in Great Britain in 2010 by:

Young Writers
Remus House
Coltsfoot Drive
Peterborough
PE2 9JX
Telephone: 01733 890066
Website: www.youngwriters.co.uk

All Rights Reserved
Book Design by Spencer Hart, Ali Smith & Tim Christian
© Copyright Contributors 2010
SB ISBN 978-1-84924-842-6

Foreword

Young Writers' Bust-A-Rhyme competition is a showcase for secondary school pupils to share their poetic creativity and inspiration. Selecting the poems has been challenging and immensely rewarding. The effort and imagination invested by these young writers makes their poems a pleasure to enjoy reading time and time again.

Young Writers was established in 1991 to nurture creativity in our children and young adults, to give them an interest in poetry and an outlet to express themselves. Seeing their work in print will encourage them to keep writing and become our poets of tomorrow.

Contents

Aireville School, Skipton
Jodie Solloway (12) 1
Francesca Nelson (12) 1
Ruth Garrett (12) 2
Matthew Smith (13) 2
Charli Hill (12) 3
Megan Louise Whitton (12) 3
Mikaela Teal (13) 4
Chloe-May Rudden (12) 4
Hannah Duke (12) 5
Kyle Lord (13) 5
James Tidswell (12) 6
Adam Brookes (13) 6
Katie Rawson (12) 7
Robert Trimble (13) 7
Demi Neave (13) 8
Jo Shakespeare (13) 8
George Sutcliffe (13) 9
Becky Milnes (12) 9

Burnside Business & Enterprise College, Wallsend
Ryan Garrett (13) 9
Ashleigh Gardner (13) 10
Adam Graham (13) 10
Stephen Jamieson (13) 11
Sarah McKenzie (13) 11
Daniel Hogarth (13) 12
Bradley Hickman (13) 12
Shannon Neve (13) 13
Darren Hamilton (13) 13
Lauren Pearl Noon Gillen (14) 14
Callum Ireland (13) 14
Harry Steanson (13) 15
Jessica Charlton (13) 15
Montanna Watson (13) 16
Joe McIntyre (13) 16
Kye Morton (13) 17
Luke Molloy (13) 17
Lauren Gosling (14) 18
Ellie Brennan (13) 18

Stefanie Fish (13) 19
Ashleigh Layburn (13) 19
Alice Rose Freeth (13) 20
Jessica Kwok (13) 20
Leanne Maddison (13) 21
Holly Muirhead 21
Jamie Rahim (13) 22
Rebecca Jayne Taylor (13) 22
Ashley Fletcher 23
Jessica Gaddes (13) 23
Dylan Tully (13) 24
Joanne Kelly (13) 24
Dane Dobson 25
Kevin Jack Costello (13) 25
Jessica Henry (13) 26
Sam Graham (13) 26
Beth Davison (13) 26
Kristian White-Harper (14) 27
Craig Burns (13) 27

Bydales School, Marske-by-the-Sea
Emily Metcalfe (12) 27
Joshua Graham (12) 28
Michael Storey (12) 28
Marcia Pryce (12) 29
Daniel Hayward (12) 29
Jenna-Beth Game (12) 30
Nathan Farrell (13) 30
Helen Gawthorpe (12) 31
Gemma Gosling (12) 31
Hayley Wilson (13) 32
Ellie Clements (12) 32
Jack Storey (12) 33
Thomas Wheatley (12) 33
Jack Buckley (13) 34
Matthew Marshall (12) 34
Bethany Lees (12) 34
Charlie Helm (13) 35
Emma Jayne Maret (13) 35

Filey School, Filey

Katherine Garbutt (13) 35
Alexander Low (14) 36
Amy Jack (13) 37
Rebeca Holmes (14) 37
Amy O'Donnell (14) 38
Olivia-Jo Lovitt (14) 39
Alexandria Nellist (14) 40
Ben Lyon 40
Ella Dobson (13) 41
Charlotte Wright (14) 41
Kate Clayton (14) 42
Lucy Butler (13) 42
Sarah Grayshan (13) 43

Hesketh Fletcher High School, Atherton

Jasmine Pendlebury Cook (11) 43
Kiana Hughes (14) 44
Tanya Clarke (14) 45
Rosie Smith (12) 46
Sarah Hargreaves (14) 47
Charlie Kim Holmes (14) 47

Marden Bridge Middle School, Whitley Bay

Abe Treumann (12) 48
Sarah MacLeod (12) 49
Josh Oxley (12) 50
Jack White (13) 50
Jake Wilson (13) 51
Lewis Boyle (12) 51
James Brookes (12) 52
Amy McCartney (12) 52
Hilly Hannam (12) 53
Jordan Robson (12) 53
Jemima Heasman (12) 54
Casey Lee Grieveson (12) 54
Jessica Dix (13) 55
Paul Lastockins (12) 55
Phoebe Watson (12) 56
Stephen Vose (12) 56
Joseph Auchterlonie (12) 57
Thomas McDonough (12) 57
Chelsea Byrne (12) 58

Bridie Munro (12) 58
James Wilson (12) 59
Amy Wilson (13) 59
Noi Jenkinson (12) 60
Rebecca Cross (12) 60
Sarah Elkin (12) 61
Daniel Atkin (12) 61
Andrew Rigg (12) 62
Hannah Gilroy (13) 62
Aaron Goldwater (12) 62
Andy Tweedy (12) 63
Raymond Tough (12) 63
Daniel David Walker (12) 63
Connor Murray (12) 64

Ripon Grammar School, Ripon

Meg Jameson-Allen (11) 64
Shannon Millar (12) 65
Edward Lyons (11) 66
Issy Gould (11) 67
Megan Aspinall (16) 67
Jessica Burgess (16) 68
Emma Beaumont (11) 68
Megan Ruth Oakeley (13) 69
Ashley Lowe (16) 69
Ashleigh Messenger (12) 70
Zack Duffy (11) 70
Michael Hasan (12) 71
Maddie Botros (12) 71
Emma Hope (11) 72
Will Andrew (11) 72
Zoë Umpleby (12) 73
Alannah Mae Mansfield (12) 73
Rebecca Boarman (11) 74
Madeleine Marston (11) 74
Lauren Bradwell (11) 75
Matthew Cotton (11) 75
Rebekah Vanzo (13) 76
Elleanor Lamb (11) 76
Sophie Charlton (12) 77
Imogen Oakes (11) 77
Jack Burgess (12) 78
Leanne Anderson (11) 78
Eleanor Duffield (16) 79
Aimee Rutherford (12) 80

Victoria Frost (11)	80
Kate Grime (11)	81
Lucy Chapman (12)	81
Jess Alice Butterell (13)	82
Heather Laws (13)	82
Sam Cooper (11)	83
Jamie Bowker (12)	83
Theo Lumsden (11)	84
Jessica Bryden (12)	84
Richard Langdale (12)	85
Tom Sladen (11)	85
Max Crompton (12)	86
Nathan Atkinson (13)	86
Anna Durkin (11)	87
Kimberley Hall (11)	87
Lewis Bartlem (11)	88
Evie Don (12)	88
Shannon Groves (11)	89
Thomas Lonsdale (11)	89
Annabelle Ayliffe (12)	90
Sophie Reed (11)	90
Nicola Terry (12)	91
Bently Briggs (12)	91
Chris Wallace (15)	92
Constance Lumsdon (11)	92
Harry Yates (13)	93
Francesca Howe (13)	93
Regan Raffle (12)	94
James Douglas Hamilton (11)	94
Abigail Ward (14)	95
Megan Lane (16)	96
Bryn May (13)	97
Calum Richardson (11)	98
Ciarán Steele (12)	99
Jack Burton (11)	100
Donna Castle-Ward (11)	100
Luke Robinson (13)	101
Henry Way (11)	101
Dashiell Barnes (13)	102
Lydia Bakes (11)	102
Hannah Scholes (12)	103
Emily Peirson (11)	103
Julia Atherley (11)	104
Sean Bartlem (11)	104
Joe Brown (12)	105
Imogen Fowler (15)	105
Sophie Veitch (12)	106
Alex Gath-Walker (16)	106
Maria Isabel Scullion (11)	107
Jessica Rutherford (12)	107
Naomi Fowler (17)	108
Thomas Bowe (11)	108
Derek Van Der Westhuizen (13)	109
Harry Cleary (11)	109
Annabelle Blyton (12)	110
Alexander Speight (13)	110
Georgina Brewer (14)	111
Jack Baker (11)	111
Holly Oldham (11)	112
James Woolfenden (14)	112
Leah Carling (12)	113
Emma Armstrong (11)	113
Peter Walker (12)	114
Matthew James Pimley (11)	114
George Robinson (12)	115
Oliver Colville (12)	115
Emily Brook (11)	116
Bethany Abel (11)	116
Elliot Fearn (11)	117
Alexander Vanzo (11)	117
Thomas Stringer (12)	118
Samuel Atkinson (11)	118
Ryan Wood (11)	119
Max Oliver Vesty (11)	119
Thomas Whitaker (12)	120
Will Forbes (16)	120
Bethanie Archer (11)	121
Emily Horner (15)	121
Tom Beaumont (11)	121
Miles Butterell (11)	122
Molly Aikman (11)	122
Daniel Williams (11)	122
Katie Treasure (11)	123
Jacob Turner (11)	123
James Andrews (11)	123

Salford City Academy, Eccles

Elizabeth Jones (12)	124
Courtney Newton (12)	125
Natasha Tomlinson (14)	126

Faye Lengden (12) 127
Nicholas Cluley (13) 127
Alexandra Cowlishaw (13) 128
Josh Farrell & James Looker (15) 128
Bethany Downie (13) 129
Saul Whittle (14) 129
Katie-Jayne Leggott (12) 130
Natalie Harwood (12) 130
Natasha Roebuck (12) 131
Kaylie Devine Williams (13) 131
Malek Abdo (12) 132
Amy Richards (13) 132
Leoni Sufyaan (13) 133
Louis Edmonds (12) 133
Melissa Louise Robinson (13) 134
Jody Entwistle (13) 134
Katie Halliwell (12) 135
Ellie Scott (14) 135
Jack Redford (12) 136
Emma Tombling (13) 136
Rochelle Johnson (13) 137
Jack Nicholson (12) 137
Daniel Edwards (12) 138

The Read School, Selby
Bryony Chapman (12) 138
Phoebe Simpson (13) 139
Katie Poskitt (11) 139
Luke Rayner (11) 140
Victoria Leigh (11) 140
Megan Victoria Hughes (12) 141
Chris Porter (13) 141
Jenny Stauffer (11) 141
Alex Tant-Brown (11) 142

Walkden High School, Worsley
Emma Farrington (12) 142
Edward Hughes (12) 143
Adam Peacock (12) 145
Amy Broome, Jenna Millership &
Amy Masters (12) 146
Jack Corrigan (13) 146

Westlands School, Thornaby
Jake Allison (13) 147
James Coates (13) 147

Joshua Waller (13) 148
Billy Hill (13) 148
Matthew Taylor (14) 148

Whickham School, Whickham
Katy Jenkins (11) 149
Francesca Louise Best (12) 150
Jennifer Thomson (12) 151
Kaitlin Sophie Fiddler (11) 152
Jack Stewart 153
Hannah Shield (14) 154
Conor Gillespie (13) 155
Daniel James Smith (12) 156
Rebecca Horsfall (11) 156
Niamh Reading (12) 157
Samantha Wynn (14) 157
Kate Farrey (12) 158
Kaylea Steadman (12) 158
Caitlin Leigh Jefferson (12) 159
Oliver Leathard (12) 159
Lucy Wallwork (13) 160
James McColl (11) 160
Emma Foster (13) 161
Niall Sutherland (11) 161
Sophie Drury (13) 162
Jordan Oloman (14) 162
Mollie Pugmire (11) 163
Callum Jones (11) 163
Ross Norman (13) 164
Elliot Anderson (12) 164
Abbey Humphreys &
Emily Higgins (13) 165
Sarah Blacklock (12) 165
Emma Crabtree (12) 166
James Thompson (11) 166
Alice Arbon (11) 167
Sophie Mansel (13) 167
Alex Luke Franklin (13) 168
Tadiwa Forster (11) 168
Jordan Hudson (13) 169
Marcus Bell (13) 169
Keir Redfern (14) 170
James Dobson (13) 170
Nathan Haley (13) 171
Nathan Johnson (11) 171

Sarah Beggs (12) 172
Elliott Shattock (12) 172
Rachel Taylor (13) 173
Caitlin Bray (13).................................... 173
George Henderson (12)........................ 174
Luke Rogers (11) 174
Francesca Riani (13) 175
Emma Martin (13)................................. 175
Bethany Lowes (12).............................. 176
Jamila Ati (11) 176
Amy Thoburn (13)................................. 177
Georgia Watkins (12)............................ 177
Samantha Ion (12)................................ 178
Shaun Angus (12) 178
Daniel Jackson (13).............................. 179
Sophie McGovern (12) 179
Emma Iveson (13) 180
Lucy Watson (12) 180
Charlotte Dunhill (11)............................ 181
Sophie Emily Turner (12)...................... 181
Lauren 182
Charlotte Birkett (11)............................. 182
Ethan Days (13).................................... 183
Shaye Little (12) 183
Thomas Fox (12) 184
Elliott Hancock (11)............................... 184
Hannah Hailes (12)............................... 185
Daniel Thomas Adams (12) 185
Anna Veitch (11) 186
Charlotte Angus (12)............................. 186
Jack Hobson (11).................................. 187
Kara Michaela Lowes (12).................... 187
Ross Walker (14) 188
James Cooney...................................... 188
Holly Robson (12)................................. 189
Megan Gates (11)................................. 189
Ellen Harrison (11)................................ 190
Michael Pottinger (12) 190
Abbie Degnan (13) 190
Robynne Clare (13).............................. 191
Kane Harm (12).................................... 191
Corey Aitchison (11) 191
Ben Gill (11).. 192
Sarah Bird (12)..................................... 192
Nicole Humphreys (11)......................... 192

The Poems

Our Two Cats

Our two cats,
They're as mad as two hats
Especially the black one.
She's grumpy, cantankerous
And ill at ease,
She sits on the sofa
And scratches her fleas.
But the ginger fella,
What can you say?
Out all night
And sleeps all day,
Sometimes you'd hear
My mother mutter,
'That naughty cat is
Licking the butter.'
Stripy tail and cheeky grin,
Too slow to catch a mouse
But still brings them in.
Our two cats,
Cuddly and cute,
One is vicious,
The other is a hoot.

Jodie Solloway (12)
Aireville School, Skipton

Everyone Does

Everyone loses someone,
Everyone does.
Everyone mourns for them,
Everyone does.
Everyone feels sad,
One way or another.
Everyone feels uncomfortable,
Everyone does.
Everyone is quiet,
Why?

Francesca Nelson (12)
Aireville School, Skipton

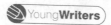

The Prisoner

Locked up in a cage
Forever and ever
Not moving
Forever and ever
Not knowing happiness
Forever and ever
A prisoner for eternity

I'll never know love
Soft grass under my feet
The gentle sounds of bird songs
The rustling of leaves
Preening myself daily
Scratching for worms
Or sunbathing under the bright blue sky

But no, I'm locked up in a cage
Forever and ever
They make me lay eggs
Forever and ever
I'll never know freedom
I'm a battery hen
Prisoner for eternity.

Ruth Garrett (12)
Aireville School, Skipton

Penguins

Penguins, penguins in black and white
Penguins, penguins you sleep at night
You sometimes skid on your belly
You don't get to eat any jelly

Penguins, penguins eating fish
Penguins, penguins, oh I wish
Just to become one of you
But I will never be able to.

Matthew Smith (13)
Aireville School, Skipton

Baahbra: My Life

Fluffy and white,
But not so bright.
I follow people around,
Bleating is my sound.

Sheepdogs put us in a herd,
A farmer whistles with his mouth,
The sheepdog chases us from north to south.
The farmer shouts, 'Sit and stay.'
In the pen no room to play.

As my lambs roam all day,
I sit and think they will not stay.
Eight more months and they will go,
To a place I do not know.

When spring comes it will happen once more,
I'll be a mother,
My lambs I'll adore.
Sheep nice but food and fun,
My lamb's circle of life has just begun.

Charli Hill (12)
Aireville School, Skipton

The Holiday

The sun, sea and the sand,
Wake up, it's time to play.
The sun, sea and the sand,
Come on, let's go this way.
The sun, sea and the sand,
Just look at those waves.
The sun, sea and the sand,
It's nearly the end of the day.
The sun has gone to bed,
The sea is all empty
And the sand has no sandcastles now.
The children have gone to bed,
Resting for another day.

Megan Louise Whitton (12)
Aireville School, Skipton

Elephants

Elephants roaming here and there,
Wandering everywhere, they don't care,
Walking everywhere in a herd,
Tails as fluffy as a bird.

Living in deserts and also in zoos,
Staying together, walking in twos,
Stomping about on their massive feet,
They always have lots of food to eat.

Lovely faces with big, flappy ears,
Their body twenty times as big as a deer's,
Their tiny tail swishes at the back,
Their bodies are nice and grey, not black.

They make people happy and also smile,
It's lovely to see elephants once in a while,
So why not go see them at the zoo?
You never know, the elephants may love you.

Mikaela Teal (13)
Aireville School, Skipton

The Snowman

Standing in the cold,
All frosty and white,
The snow falls down
To his delight,
Just to stay there,
For one more night,
He doesn't want to disappear
Before the morning light.

Carrot for his nose,
Top hat standing tall,
Scarf around his neck
Waiting for the kids to come and play
Before he goes away.
Snowman . . .

Chloe-May Rudden (12)
Aireville School, Skipton

My Seed

A tiny little seed
Needing to grow.
I picked it up
And took it home.
I fed it some water,
I gave it some sun.

And then one day
I saw petals!
It grew and grew
And grew and grew,
And no one was to know
That the seed I picked up
Was always mine,
And that I made it grow.

Hannah Duke (12)
Aireville School, Skipton

Don't Ruin The World

If you ruin the world it will be horrible to see
And yes, it will affect both you and me,
The trees won't be green,
There will be no good scene,
The animals will die,
We would have to say goodbye.
The pollution would mean,
The air would not be clean,
The sea would be grey,
So would every day,
So if we don't act fast,
The world will not last,
The world would just fall,
It would kill us all.

Kyle Lord (13)
Aireville School, Skipton

Friendly Fish

Fish swim in the sea,
Swimming very happily,
Enjoying life like you and me,
I'd rather be a fish than a bee.

All beautiful and different types of fish,
Cats will eat them out of a dish,
For children to have a fish as a wish,
Big, fat, small and round fish.

So this is my pet fish
Who swims around in a dish,
It came true, did my wish,
Eventually, when I got my pet fish.

James Tidswell (12)
Aireville School, Skipton

The Tiger

The tiger runs through the jungle,
Catching its prey, landing in a bundle,
Eating meat with its cubs
And resting next to some shrubs.

The tiger licks its paws,
It doesn't have to do chores,
Catching food for its babies
And attracting lots of tiger ladies.

The tiger is sleeping on the African plains,
One of the things he'd never change,
Ripping apart the gazelle's meat,
Giving his cubs a big treat.

Adam Brookes (13)
Aireville School, Skipton

Nature's Seasons

All the autumn colours,
The cold winter freeze,
The flowers that belong to spring,
The cooling summer breeze.

The seasons belongs to nature,
To the tree, animal and bird,
The world belongs to everything,
Or so I've heard.

But I've heard of global warming
And the litter weighing a ton,
We need to look after our Earth,
But remember . . . have fun.

Katie Rawson (12)
Aireville School, Skipton

Sister

I have a little sister,
She's really quite a pain,
There are some times when I just wish
She'd get hit by a train.

And then she gets real noisy
And never stops to think,
Of what would happen, if she trips
And falls into the sink.

I do have one good memory
Of which I'm rather fond,
Of when she ran around and round
And fell into the pond.

Robert Trimble (13)
Aireville School, Skipton

Vampire Love

Motionless, there I stand
I'm drowning in the darkness
Your intense, evil eyes gaze into mine
Fully mesmerised
I speak coldly, 'I'm just a heartless vampire'
My bleeding neck makes me want you more
Still I crave, crave that taste again
With the onset, like slashes wound deeply
Love is not when you feel only pain
These fangs, like knives on my neck
My skin prickles
This blood on my hands.

Demi Neave (13)
Aireville School, Skipton

My Split Ends

M irror, mirror on the wall . . .
Y uk!

S plit ends,
P ain in the neck,
L ook disgusting.
I need some help,
T o the hairdressers!

'E lp!
N eed the scissors,
D rastic measures,
S nip, snip!

Jo Shakespeare (13)
Aireville School, Skipton

Rugby

Rugby is brilliant, rugby is great
Letting out all of your bottled hate
Still play by the rules
Yet managing to nail
Winning and losing
Not much the same
Being a sportsman
Yet feeling ashamed
Whether sending someone to hospital
Or scoring the winning try
Rugby always leaves you with your head held high.

George Sutcliffe (13)
Aireville School, Skipton

Buds

A dead flower bed
There grows a bud
Only small.
It stretches for the light
Pushing away the earth.
Growing, growing, growing.
The small bud, now a big rose.

Becky Milnes (12)
Aireville School, Skipton

Lights

It's late at night.
The time is right.
I have imagined loads of lights.
They started to flash a crazy red,
But I don't know how in front of me it goes so white.
Then I recognise people sprinting out of this black light.
Then I realise I am in a war.

Ryan Garrett (13)
Burnside Business & Enterprise College, Wallsend

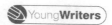

Just Another Family

A family is the most important thing in life,
For anyone, well for me it is.
Although I'm not as close to them
As the Jacksons, or some other famous family are,
I won't pretend I am - there have been plenty of fall-outs
Over serious issues and things that just don't matter.
Maybe it could be some simple issue like,
'Who's going shopping?'
So mostly the arguments mean nothing.
Then there are the times we spend together,
The memories we all share,
When all the aunties and uncles remember
When they used to spend every summer day in the back lane.
They never fail to question me and my cousins,
'Why do you waste time on the computer,
You should be playing outside in the sun shouldn't you?'
But you must excuse them, they still think it's 1973,
According to my ancient uncle, the music isn't 'real' nowadays,
He says that while he sticks on his Beatles records.
But all my family is just another brick in the wall,
But they're as good as any family can get,
They're fine, just as they are.

Ashleigh Gardner (13)
Burnside Business & Enterprise College, Wallsend

The Truth

I sit alone at night and shiver,
With the footsteps on the stairs.
They get closer and closer,
The goosebumps appear.
The door opens slowly
With a scary screech,
They both come in.
I know what is about to happen.
In the morning the bruises and images,
They shall haunt me forever.

Adam Graham (13)
Burnside Business & Enterprise College, Wallsend

Untitled

I was walking through the park one day
When I came upon a bench
A dog came up beside me
Who had an awful stench

I was walking through the street one day
When I came upon a wall
I was gong to sit on it
But I thought I would fall

I was walking through the field one day
When I came upon a farmer
I stopped and talked to him
And he couldn't have been calmer

I was walking through my house one day
When I came upon a spider
I didn't run away
And the spider didn't either

When I stop and think, I walked about a lot
I saw a lot of things and met a lot of people
Now I'm home, I'm tired
And now I am going to sleep.

Stephen Jamieson (13)
Burnside Business & Enterprise College, Wallsend

Best Holiday

I went to Scotland for a week
I loved the sound, the sight, the sheep.
Everything seemed alright, until my friend got into a fight,
After that we had a chat.
Never again to feel the same
About those people I loved.
When I got home too upset to talk
You'll be confused.
But the time I went through
Led to the best holiday ever.

Sarah McKenzie (13)
Burnside Business & Enterprise College, Wallsend

I Hate Chavs!

I hate chavs because
They do drugs
They smoke
And they listen to MC

I hate chavs because
Of their language
They loiter
And they start fights with you

I hate chavs because
They bully
They think they're hard
And they're *loud!*

I hate chavs because
They're annoying
They think everyone should do what they want
And they're criminals

I hate chavs because
They care about no one but themselves
They hang around in parks
And that's why I hate chavs!

Daniel Hogarth (13)
Burnside Business & Enterprise College, Wallsend

Bust-A-Rhyme

It is the time
To bust a rhyme
So let's rap to the beat
And dance with your feet
In comes the DJ to rock this place
The party's not going to be a disgrace
You need to get out on your feet
To rock to the beat
Get on the dance floor
That's the end of a show.

Bradley Hickman (13)
Burnside Business & Enterprise College, Wallsend

No One But You . . .

You're sitting on your doorstep,
You've been kicked out of your house,
You decide to walk down your street,
But no one is around.

You don't know what you've done
To deserve all this nonsense,
Everyone thinks badly of you,
Your parents think you're a nuisance.

Words cannot describe
How you feel right now.
Your mother's just abused you
And all you said was, 'Ow.'

Your dad comes out looking for you,
You can hear his drunken voice,
You don't want to go back to them,
You can't stand all the noise.

You're homeless, you're scared,
You don't know what to do,
There's no one to help you,
No one but you.

Shannon Neve (13)
Burnside Business & Enterprise College, Wallsend

When I Grow Up

When I grow up, things begin to change
When I grow up, this is called age
When I grow up, I get bigger
When I grow up, my job will be driving a digger
When I grow up I could get spots
When I grow up I don't want lots
When I grow up, I'll have to do things alone
When I grow up, I'll be accident prone
All this is me, when I grow up.

Darren Hamilton (13)
Burnside Business & Enterprise College, Wallsend

Unconditional Love

The unconditional love of a parent,
It's hard to explain, but true,
From when you are born,
Even when you die,
This love shall never leave you.
Through thick times and thin times,
Through the gentle and rough,
Through all times
They'll be there,
No matter how tough.
The unconditional love of a parent,
Biological or not,
They'll feed you,
Care for you,
Stand by you, no matter what.
This pair, they're quite fantastic you know,
Between them they share no greed,
Here for you forever,
For you and siblings alone,
The unconditional love of a parent,
That's all you ever need.

Lauren Pearl Noon Gillen (14)
Burnside Business & Enterprise College, Wallsend

School Poem

School is boring and very bad
That's why I am really sad.
No fun, no free time,
Always working all the time.
School in the morning is very boring,
Being in the house is a big disgrace.
Homework, no fun, no free time,
Always working all the time.
On the back of the bus,
Just the two of us.
PE is the best, forget the rest.

Callum Ireland (13)
Burnside Business & Enterprise College, Wallsend

Ascendancy

As you see the rotting skyline
The Earth focuses amongst the twilight,
Prime candidate, world on my shoulders,
Then it crushes down, two tonne boulders.
This life ravages, yet happy,
Joyful, yet sad,
Pool of emotions, happy and glad
It can turn to danger and mud.
Fascism and Christianity, they don't go.
World evaporating, immensely slow.
Shrine of pollution, focus our eyes,
Soon to be our last goodbyes
Smile, smile,
For miles and miles,
If you're engaged on this life,
You'd know it's like the blade of a knife.
Sun beams down, through and through
And look up, smiles on you!

Harry Steanson (13)
Burnside Business & Enterprise College, Wallsend

Untitled

Yesterday was fun
Today is hard
Tomorrow is still to come

The day is through
The finish of all work
But tomorrow there's more to do

A break would be fine
But four more days to go
Is the time I like to call mine

To other people that go there
Like all the kids I know
To me it seems like they don't care
About which mark they'll get.

Jessica Charlton (13)
Burnside Business & Enterprise College, Wallsend

Most Important

The most important is Mother
She lives in a nice, light bubble
My cat comes next
And likes to text
Then it's the grandmother and father
She's a gardener and he's a farmer

Then it's my sister
Who talks like a mister
Next comes Fudge, the big brown bear
He's really a horse, but don't tell, *you dare!*
My aunts and uncles come now
Who like to argue and row

Me? I'm simple
I have a dimple
I love my family but I love my pets more
I have to go
There's a knock at the door.

Montanna Watson (13)
Burnside Business & Enterprise College, Wallsend

Untitled

The people shouting all around, their words hitting like bombs.
People staring at one another, trying to watch each other.
Why do they stare?
Why do they look?
Why do some of them snigger?
Why? Because I'm smart, or because I'm easy pickings.
All I know, is that it really hurts my feelings.
Some people like their fists to hurt,
Some people use their feet,
But others use their words of pain
Which hurt me worst of all.
I hope it will stop, I pray it will end,
But all I know is this,
Please stop the hurtful calling.

Joe McIntyre (13)
Burnside Business & Enterprise College, Wallsend

Your Friends

You can always rely on them.
No matter how bad the situation is,
They will always solve it for you in the end.
These times will be the best times of your life.
Funny times, happy times, sad times and scary times.
Which times were the best times in your teenage life?
But when they turn on you
You will not know what to do,
It will feel like you're all on your own,
Until you see the crack of dawn,
Then they will come to you,
They say they are sorry,
As they're your friends, you always forgive them.
What would the world be like without friends?
I know, and it's the worst thing in your life,
So respect your friends
And they'll respect you.

Kye Morton (13)
Burnside Business & Enterprise College, Wallsend

So What!

So what if I never score goals often?
Doesn't mean I'm bad.
So what if I am tackled?
Doesn't mean they're better than me.
So what if I am in a better team than some?
Doesn't mean that people can call me.
So what if people are jealous?
So what if we win? It isn't the end.
So what if you don't start?
Doesn't mean you can't battle back to do so.
So what if you get beat?
Doesn't it mean you can't get better.
This is my life in football and this has happened.
I wish it would go away but what can you do?
My name is Luke Molloy and that's my story.

Luke Molloy (13)
Burnside Business & Enterprise College, Wallsend

At Least I Can Always Trust Them

You'll always have a best friend
No matter what your age
Old or young, it doesn't matter
They'll stand by you anyway

There may be a time
When your best friends turn to you
With problems of their own
And they don't know what to do
You'll listen really carefully
And offer your advice
They will thank you for that

You can share your hobbies with them
Or go to see a film
And maybe have a sleepover, or two
Cos I'll always have a best friend
And at least I can always trust them.

Lauren Gosling (14)
Burnside Business & Enterprise College, Wallsend

Life Is A Roller Coaster

Life is a roller coaster
Up and down, side to side
Then, just when you start to think
All the problems stop,
You look ahead at the track
And then a plunge into darkness.
You tighten your grip
Ready for the big drop.

'Is it over?
Is my life finished?'
I wait, too scared to open my eyes.
I can see a light, a bright light.
1, 2, 3, *open!*
Daylight, back to the normal world,
Cold, polluted and swirled.

Ellie Brennan (13)
Burnside Business & Enterprise College, Wallsend

Tears In The Rain

The sheeting rain falls against the window.
Is it crying someone else's tears, or my own?
But I can't get out
To delve into someone else's worries;
And, somehow forget about my own.

It isn't my tear stained pillow that lies beneath my head
And as I hide my face under your quilt,
Your stone eyes come to my memory.
Will I ever see your eyes again?
And then I wonder . . .

I stand at the window,
Watching hundreds of tears fall.
I wish I were out there with you,
But you're not in my sight.
For all I can see are grey clouds.

Stefanie Fish (13)
Burnside Business & Enterprise College, Wallsend

Being Shy

She thinks you're a horrible person
Just because you're shy.
The sly comments,
You wanna drift away with clouds.

Running faster every time
In case she catches you before the bus
Screaming, 'Come back for a fight!'
You stop to a halt,
She pulls your hair,
Thinking she's well hard in front of her mates.
As hard as she could be, she doesn't care.
The anger builds up and up,
You swing for her.
She's out of the scene in one blow.
Violence is not the way!

Ashleigh Layburn (13)
Burnside Business & Enterprise College, Wallsend

He Never Came

As I stood there in the rain
Waiting, waiting for someone who never came.
In the dark, there I wait, for the person who never came.
Slowly the sun rose, like a ball of fire in the sky
But he still never came.
Next day, still waiting
The dark, misty moon replaced the sun
And he still never came.
I continued to wait and still I was alone.
Then, I realised he would never come
So I gave up waiting.
The day I dreaded most came
He would not come.
He was no longer mine.
I wish I'd waited for the guy who never came.

Alice Rose Freeth (13)
Burnside Business & Enterprise College, Wallsend

What I Love And Like . . .

I like being happy
I love my family
I like playing on my laptop
I love to listen to music (Korean, Chinese, English)
I like chatting to friends
I love to smile and make people smile
I like spending time with my family and friends
I love shopping
I like designing things
I love to watch Asian dramas
I like to laugh
I love *cupcakes* (so cute!)
I like sweets
But I don't like school.

Jessica Kwok (13)
Burnside Business & Enterprise College, Wallsend

Helpless

Every night up in my room,
I hear the noises so loud and full,
But who will be there to help them when
The bruises and bite marks are covered then?
The horrible truth is this isn't the only one,
The horrible truth is it hasn't just begun.
You see, this happens all the time
And all they wish is just to die.
No one should have to put up with this,
All the hurt and pain.
See, I don't know what to do, I'm only a kid.
Should I tell my parents about it?
I'm scared in case it happens to me,
But I know my mum and dad love me.

Leanne Maddison (13)
Burnside Business & Enterprise College, Wallsend

I'll Get By

I suppose it's just karma
That's what they say
What goes around comes around
That's just his way.

Maybe I'll see him again
But that's just absurd
It's impossible to be okay
Seen or even heard.

I'm still just learning
The ways of life
I'm still incredulous
But I'm strong
I'll get by.

Holly Muirhead
Burnside Business & Enterprise College, Wallsend

Alone

He walked through the playground, walking all alone
He used to have many friends, but now he has none
He used to be liked by many, but now he's liked by none

'Stupid nerd' and 'teacher's pet', words whispered behind his back
Words like daggers to stab deep into his heart

No one talks to him for fear of being uncool
He thinks, *who would make such a rule?*

He's pushed around by other boys
As if he's one of their toys

There are others who are like him
But he's sure he's the worst
Standing alone in this unfriendly world.

Jamie Rahim (13)
Burnside Business & Enterprise College, Wallsend

Why?

Hiding behind corners, trying to hide your face.
You're just not like the others.
Walking through school and streets
Staring down at your feet.
People look and people laugh,
And kick you right in the back.
People don't see how you feet at night,
All alone, with no family in sight.
No one to talk to, no one to help you,
Just want out of this terrible mess.
Your parents have left you,
You're now by yourself,
With no money to start paying the rent.

Rebecca Jayne Taylor (13)
Burnside Business & Enterprise College, Wallsend

My Dad

Back to the day when my dad was around,
No one ever made a sound.
He looked so pale, so skinny and sick,
It went so silent we could hear the clock tick.

As we helped him out of bed,
We looked at each other, we were so scared.
He went to hospital, he could not eat,
All we could do was take a seat.

Now he is not here anymore,
With all his favourite things we filled a drawer.
As I say, 'I wish you were still here.'
In my eye appears a tear.

Ashley Fletcher
Burnside Business & Enterprise College, Wallsend

The Poem Of My Life

Life, life so boring and plain,
Parents, parents they drive me insane.
Chavs, chavs they make me feel sick,
Plastics, plastics, make-up so thick.

Friends, friends they make my life fun,
So joyful and happy as bright as the sun.
Kay, Ay, Emm, Bee, Enn
Make me laugh again and again.

Going out, going out, western to sporty
We're not these people who're solid and naughty
Photos, photos so random and silly
My friends are my life, and so is my Billy.

Jessica Gaddes (13)
Burnside Business & Enterprise College, Wallsend

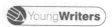

I Like

I like skating, there's so much to learn,
I like basketball, it's fun,
I like music, it keeps me calm,
I like video games, from night till dawn.

I like sweets, so much taste,
I like chilling, it calms me down,
I like my brother, he is so funny,
I like my sister, she takes away my frown.

I like my mam, she cares for me,
I like my dad, he helps me with stuff,
I like my family, they love me loads,
I like poetry, but it's so, so tough.

Dylan Tully (13)
Burnside Business & Enterprise College, Wallsend

Someone Inside

She's had enough of bullies,
She's all alone,
Even at home,
Because no one understands her fully.

She's got her life planned out,
But she's got doubt.
She sits in the corner,
Still feeling smaller,
Her bullies are coming out.

But someone inside her has opened a door,
She's stronger than those bullies before.
Now they will leave her alone.

Joanne Kelly (13)
Burnside Business & Enterprise College, Wallsend

Kid A

I'm not the person who would go and stab
Although I might if I don't get my tabs
I've got a mint car, it's pure green
Got caught with wacky in my windscreen
I got arrested just for the night
Then the police tried to start a fight
I boffed out his teeth
But he was the chief
He pulled out his taser
And blinded me with his laser
See, I won't stab, I just punch
But you better watch out when I'm with my bunch.

Dane Dobson
Burnside Business & Enterprise College, Wallsend

Clock

Is time, is time, is time
Is a good time to rhyme
People know my name
And people play my game.

Is time, is time, is time
Is a good time to rhyme
I know there's a spirit called love
And there's a bird called a dove.

Is time, is time, is time
Is a good time to rhyme.

Kevin Jack Costello (13)
Burnside Business & Enterprise College, Wallsend

Untitled

I don't want to grow old, weak and frail
Whilst at the same time I don't want to fail.
I want to do the best I can in life.
This doesn't make me a nerd, for trying my best.
Life's too short,
By the time I have fulfilled my dream,
My life is at an end.
I'll do my best,
Until I become old, weak and frail.

Jessica Henry (13)
Burnside Business & Enterprise College, Wallsend

A Winter Poem

Cold winter's night, snowy delight.
Snowball fights, cold nights.
Make snow angels, going sledding.
Lovely warm bedding.
I love these snowy nights.
White sky, snow piled high.
Big white snowmen like still soldiers,
As big as boulders.
That's why I love winter nights.

Sam Graham (13)
Burnside Business & Enterprise College, Wallsend

Friendship Was Wealth

She thought her friendship was strong
She found out she was wrong
She hoped it would never end
She wished she never sent
The text she wrote
She found them in her coat.

Beth Davison (13)
Burnside Business & Enterprise College, Wallsend

Bat

There was a rat with the wings of a bat
His best friend was Pat, she had a furry cat who lay on the mat.
Her cat was a lazy cat
Who hated to chase the rat,
That rat with wings like a bat.

Kristian White-Harper (14)
Burnside Business & Enterprise College, Wallsend

Laziness

Lazy is a busy business, but not all can do it.
Lazy is a tiring business, maybe you should try it.
Lazy is hard work, the work could actually kill you.
Laziness is me and you, everyone loves it.
Laziness is skilful, but only a few do it.

Craig Burns (13)
Burnside Business & Enterprise College, Wallsend

The Mind Of Dance!

Dancing is my life.
I savour it every day.
The outfits are fab.

Modern, ballet, tap,
Silent, effective great steps.
I adore them so.

Everyone dances.
Also trees dance in the wind,
Swaying left to right.

Moving gracefully,
The effect it has is priceless.
You have to love dance!

Emily Metcalfe (12)
Bydales School, Marske-by-the-Sea

Love Of Fishing

Nine o'clock I open my eyes
I bait my hooks
I sort my flies.

A lovely day for catching fish.
I step on the docks
I make a wish.

I cast a spinner,
I hook a fish,
I feel like a winner.

My rod's shaking as it's fighting.
I catch the fish,
It's so exciting.

Joshua Graham (12)
Bydales School, Marske-by-the-Sea

My Favourite Place

M y favourite place
 I s in the north-east of England
D reaming of the attractions
D oing my favourite things
 L ooking in the shops
E ating my lunch
S hop, shop, shop
B oro' football game
R ide on the bus
O ff to the shops again
U nder and over the Transporter Bridge
G oing on the big, long train
H ome time at last.

Michael Storey (12)
Bydales School, Marske-by-the-Sea

Early Morning

Early morning, I'm blue.
Early mornings sneak up on you.
Early mornings are too bright, that's true,
Like a torch in a dark tunnel.
Early mornings, I get cross with you.
Why am I more tired than when I went to bed?
Stay out of my way.
Groaning, grumbling, getting up early,
Alarms whining to keep me awake.
Would you turn them off, for goodness sake?
Tick, tick goes the clock,
It's time to go,
Do you have to get ready so, so slow?

Marcia Pryce (12)
Bydales School, Marske-by-the-Sea

February Frost

As I step on the grass,
It crunches in front of and behind me.
The sun and the ice turn us into giants.
The cold frost and ice is so slippery,
It's like I'm in a world of ice, skating.
The snow is soft,
It's like a silky mattress.
The white leaves on the trees
Are at war with the ice.
You can feel and taste
The coldness in your body.
Frost is part of nature,
But to me it's just another happening.

Daniel Hayward (12)
Bydales School, Marske-by-the-Sea

The Endangered

The tigers are slowly moving
And all the birds are scared and flying
The tiger's cubs are sitting there crying
Because the cubs' mom is dying

The rhinos are going
Because of their horns
They're being hunted to the ground
And left to die in bushes with thorns

The marine turtle used to swim
But now he floats
Because he choked
On the litter we left behind.

Jenna-Beth Game (12)
Bydales School, Marske-by-the-Sea

On My Own

Riding down the road one day,
Me, my bike and I,
Turning round so I don't stray,
Me, my bike and I.

On my own I'm so, so cold,
My bike, the wind and I.
Rusty and broken because it's old,
My bike, the wind and I.

Relaxing nicely in my car,
My heater, my drink and I.
I'm tired, I'm sweaty, I don't need to go far,
My heater, my drink and I.

Nathan Farrell (13)
Bydales School, Marske-by-the-Sea

A Ride Along The Countryside

I love riding on my bike,
It makes me feel so free.
I can forget about everything else,
Just bike, and road, and me.

I like riding off the road
On tracks in the countryside,
Riding over hill and dale
And enjoying landscapes wide.

Over jumps and bumps we fly along,
My bike is my best friend.
She never breaks or lets me down
From morning till day's end.

Helen Gawthorpe (12)
Bydales School, Marske-by-the-Sea

Trees

Oh trees, you open up your generous hands,
Leaning out as if holding a wand.
Up in your branches birds are weaving,
Ready for the day they will be leaving.

Oh trees, you welcome them in your home,
Sheltering them from the weather's demon.
The coldness and the dampness
Of rain pouring down.

Oh trees, your trunk, your roots are anchored to the ground,
Giving reassurance to all the creatures all around
Looking for food or shelter from the ground.
Trees are so special to me.

Gemma Gosling (12)
Bydales School, Marske-by-the-Sea

The Great Battle

The dry walls crumble upon touch,
The birds fall silent
And the wind drops.
I walk through the doorway,
Sword held high,
I ready my shield
And lead my army into battle.
We cry out loud to scare our foe.

The wind comes back,
The birds sing,
My armour and army vanish.
Only I will remember the great battle.

Hayley Wilson (13)
Bydales School, Marske-by-the-Sea

Growing Up

They start off very small
And become very tall.
I thought I should let you know
How I feel about it all.
As I sit I watch them grow,
Play like angels in the cold, white snow.
I think to myself about when
I was small before.
So we should treasure these moments
Before it's too late,
Soon come the wrinkles
That I shall hate.

Ellie Clements (12)
Bydales School, Marske-by-the-Sea

The Black Sea

The black sea pounds at the endless cliff
Making it more of a rocky abyss.

The black sea charges at the shaking cliff
It charges faster, wanting to crush it.

As the black sea fiercely charges on
The Herculean cliff will soon be gone.

The massive cliff is slowly falling,
The sea then lashes at it, roaring.

The cliff is now completely condemned.
I knew that malevolent sea would be its end.

Jack Storey (12)
Bydales School, Marske-by-the-Sea

Grandma

I am sad
And also mad.
We found her with her arms spread,
She was, in fact, dead.
She ascended to the heavens
At about quarter-past eleven.
She never committed any sins
And she always took out her bins.
She was very special in every way,
I miss her every single day.

Thomas Wheatley (12)
Bydales School, Marske-by-the-Sea

Edward

The high-flying buildings of New York,
Twin Towers, tumbled.
No light illuminates their place,
It's dark, dark as a black bird at night!

During the day the busy streets of New York
Bustle and rustle with the sound of
Taxis, cars and hot dog vendors called Edward,
Dressed in weenie costumes.
The mustard's as yellow as the sun at noon!

Jack Buckley (13)
Bydales School, Marske-by-the-Sea

Football Hooliganism

Football hooliganism is a very bad thing,
It happens a lot when the ball's on the wing.
The referee blows for a trip from behind,
The crowd starts shouting that he must be blind.
The ball goes flying right into the net,
The fans are all fuming, you've got to bet.
Football hooliganism is a very bad thing,
It happens a lot when the ball's on the wing.

Matthew Marshall (12)
Bydales School, Marske-by-the-Sea

Animals

A nimals of the world hear me call
N o smooth edges on coral under the sea
I nside her nest I can hear young calling me
M ammals to invertebrates, I love them all
A ll corners of the Earth, animals to call their own
L eaping off rocks with their coats
S ilent to watch them catch their prey.

Bethany Lees (12)
Bydales School, Marske-by-the-Sea

The Beaver

He beavers around in the gentle, cool water
Chomping on the gorgeous green leaves and grass
Floating on through the riverbank.

His wife swims after him
Failing to keep up.
The beaver tears on through.

Charlie Helm (13)
Bydales School, Marske-by-the-Sea

My Brother

It was a cold night like any other
When they came for my brother.
They stood there in white coats,
Some might think they looked like ghosts.
Tall and slender,
Probably of the male gender.

Emma Jayne Maret (13)
Bydales School, Marske-by-the-Sea

Confusion!

I am endlessly confused
I want a moment when
My hopes and dreams come true
And my memories just go away.

I want to cry when my love
For someone destroys my friendship.
I want to smile and to be happy forever
Instead of suddenly arguing over nothing and no one.

Crying over words that should not affect my soul.
I want to change and to be free
For that's what I want to be:
For my dreams will soon come true . . .
I hope.

Katherine Garbutt (13)
Filey School, Filey

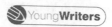

A Snowy Day At Boars Rock

Snowy hilltops
Eagles soar above
Snow lies thick
At Boars Rock.

The old, run-down houses
Foundations tattered and torn
Crofts are beautiful
At Boars Rock.

The McLaren children play
Their scarves wave in the wind
The snow covers their footprints
At Boars Rock.

The burns run clear
Their water icy cold
The snow creates no obstacle
At Boars Rock.

A school left dormant
No children inside
A playground covered with ice and snow
At Boars Rock.

An army of snowmen
Their noses bright orange
Their jackets show a tartan
At Boars Rock.

Alexander Low (14)
Filey School, Filey

Please Understand!

Please understand me
You don't know how I feel
Please understand me
You don't know what I think
Please understand me
I don't want to awaken
Please understand me
I don't know what to do
Please understand me
I don't know how to help
Please understand me
You don't know how difficult it is

Please understand me
I haven't got a clue
Please understand me
This makes no sense
Please understand me
Why did you do that?
Please understand me
Let me do what I want
Please understand me
I hate him so much
Please understand me
I liked him more than you ever did.

Amy Jack (13)
Filey School, Filey

I Have A Dream

I have a dream,
A dream to be with you.
I long for you,
I sing about you,
I talk about you.
I have a dream,
And that's just to be with you.

Rebeca Holmes (14)
Filey School, Filey

National Heart

One family
One heart
They've got the key
Champions together
Are ECT

They are proud
They are family
Full of spirit

See their energy
See their power
Together they are
One national heart

Working amongst each other
Day by day
To achieve and show
Consistent passion.

That's right, they were there
Chanting loud
'Come on, Tigers,
Show your ground!'

Amy O'Donnell (14)
Filey School, Filey

Lost

Hoping to be found
By a human or anything that makes a sound
All I can see is the deep blue sea
Is anyone going to find me?

Looking for something to eat
But I can't bear the heat
Even if I shout and scream
I don't think I will be seen.

SOS I write in stones
But no one is going to hear the moans
I am on this island, all on my own
Sat on the rocks like a king on his throne

What is this I see?
A ship sailing across the sea
It's turning the other way
I look in dismay

I am lost
Never to be found.

Olivia-Jo Lovitt (14)
Filey School, Filey

Age

Getting older is confusing
Parties at the weekend
Going out on a weekday
And yeah, it is fun!
But exhausting at the same time.

Sometimes you just want it to go back
The way it was when you were a child
Everything being perfect
Not having to worry about anything!

It is good now though
Looking forward to going out
Meeting new people
Travelling to different places.

I can imagine getting older as well
Racing around in our cars
Even more parties!
Yeah, it sounds good
But there will be even more worry.

Alexandria Nellist (14)
Filey School, Filey

Prayer For The World

Food for everyone
Clean water for everyone
Clothes for everyone
I am an adult of the future
Girls *and* boys go to school
Listen to children
Learn to be nice
Learn not to kill
Yes, end global warming
Protect animals in their habitats
(Abolish older sisters)
Justice and fairness
Honest politicians.

Ben Lyon
Filey School, Filey

Being A Teenager

Being a teenager means:
Endless confusion.
My hopes are changing.
The arguing begins.
Wishing you were invisible,
Waiting for a moment when
My hopes and dreams come true.
Happiness and sadness seem
To merge into one.
Trying to remember any good memories,
That now seem so far away.
Words hurt more than ever.
Friendships bringing happiness
When you are down.
All my beliefs in people are changing.
The weather affects my mood.
Crying is my daily schedule.
Hoping to be wanted by friends.

Ella Dobson (13)
Filey School, Filey

My Best Friend

Every night when I go home
I sit and talk,
She just sits there and listens.

I know that she probably
Doesn't understand me,
But I don't mind that.

Good or bad,
She sits and listens
To whatever I say.

I love her so much,
She is my closest friend.
I love my black cat.

Charlotte Wright (14)
Filey School, Filey

Untitled

Girls excited and giggling,
Deep down,
Overcome with nerves.
Dressed up smartly,
Shining pink and white,
Lining up to perform.
Ballerinas everywhere,
In turn, all chatty and scared,
Ready to dance on
The bright, floodlit stage.
We looked like elegant fairies
Twisting and turning,
Adrenaline pumping through our bodies
As the stage lights burned.
The audience clapped and cheered,
We curtseyed and bowed.
Feeling so proud and happy,
We scampered offstage.

Kate Clayton (14)
Filey School, Filey

Your Hopes

The hopes, the dreams,
Keep them close to you -
Little or large,
Ambitious or timid.

Sing and dance for thousands
Applauding your every move
Win for your favourite team
Hearing the roar of your name!

Achieve the grades you want
Hold close that special someone
Your hopes, your dreams
They're yours; hold them tight.

Lucy Butler (13)
Filey School, Filey

Dream Of Life

Everybody has hopes and dreams
It could be performing at the West End
Or fighting for people's rights.
Whatever the dream
Anyone can do it.
Don't let the world tell you what to do
Do what you want to do.
Whatever makes you smile -
Whatever makes you laugh -
Follow the dream.
The feeling of success
Is the feeling of the world.
There will be uphill times:
Times filled with joy -
Never forget your dream.

Sarah Grayshan (13)
Filey School, Filey

High School Rush!

People waiting in silence, waiting for the bell,
Hands sweating, tables quaking, as knees are shaking.
Slam! Smash! go the chairs,
As the bell rings for home,
People swinging their bags, upon their backs,
Standing behind their chairs.
Teachers saying, 'Class dismissed,' then it starts to shake,
The floor moves in excitement, as feet shuffle out.
The door so narrow we do not have a doubt,
That we will get stuck.
Some people laughing, some in pain,
Yelping, as they go downstairs.
I don't think people care,
The people in the corridor shouting at one another,
I don't think I will get home until next year or another!

Jasmine Pendlebury Cook (11)
Hesketh Fletcher High School, Atherton

Imagine Being Me

I slowly got up, I then got dressed,
I went down for breakfast, my mum was very impressed.
She drove me to school
In her bright yellow car,
It seemed like it took for ages,
But school wasn't really that far.
I walked into the school entrance,
I looked around for my friends.
I remembered I hadn't got any,
My life was coming to an end.
I walked along the corridor,
Someone from behind me gave me a push.
I ended up breaking my new glasses,
And dropping all my books.
I scooped them back up,
And sat down in my class.
The boy next to me gave me a nudge,
And I banged my head into the glass.
Blood dripped down my face,
I was very upset.
I tried to hold back the tears,
If I didn't I knew it would be something I would regret.
The bell went,
And it was time for lunch.
I queued up in the canteen,
A girl picked on me and gave me a punch.
I sat in my last lesson,
And I got covered in squirty foam.
The bell went, and I walked out of school,
Then I quickly ran home.

Kiana Hughes (14)
Hesketh Fletcher High School, Atherton

Imagine A World . . .

Imagine a world without parents,
You could be wild, young and free.
Imagine a world without expectations,
You could be whoever you wanted to be.
Imagine a world without sadness,
Happiness all around.
Imagine a world without restrictions,
Nowhere could be out of bound.
Imagine a world without time,
You could stay out as long as you wanted.
Imagine a world without bullies,
No one hated or taunted.
Imagine a world without difference,
Everybody would be the same.
Imagine a world without pride,
No one to disgrace and no one to shame.
Imagine a world without gravity,
Nothing holding us down.
Imagine a world without racism,
It wouldn't matter if you were white, black or brown.
Imagine a world full of peace,
No wars started at all.
Imagine a world without holes,
Nowhere for you to fall.
Imagine a world without death,
You could live as long as forever.
Imagine a world full of confidence
People would never say never.
Imagine a world without people,
Imagine a world without you, without me . . .

Tanya Clarke (14)
Hesketh Fletcher High School, Atherton

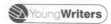

I Love You

Why did it end?
I miss the time we spend
As my heart begins to bleed
You're the only person I need
As tears run down my cheeks
I can hardly begin to speak
I'm feeling so much pain
You're driving me insane
I wish you loved me
Like the way it used to be
I wanna be by your side
Now I die a little more inside
You just don't care
Not even the memories we share
You hate my guts you say
So I cry, day by day
These are my feelings I have to express
Unloved, alone, sadness, depressed
I hate having heartbreak
For goodness sake
My love for you I can't explain
Can we try it once again?
I can't help but cry
I couldn't forget you if I tried
I love you . . .

Rosie Smith (12)
Hesketh Fletcher High School, Atherton

Love

Love is something you can't taste, hear, touch, smell,
You can see love,
Feel it,
You know when you have found it,
Something to hold on to, changes your life forever.
One person can make a difference,
You feel overjoyed, over the moon,
Happy, delighted, ecstatic,
On cloud nine.
But sometimes you feel,
Upset, sad,
Angry, distraught,
Miserable,
But love conquers all.

Sarah Hargreaves (14)
Hesketh Fletcher High School, Atherton

Does He Love Me Or Love Me Not?

Wake up early in the morning just to do my hair
He doesn't even notice, he doesn't even care.
I try to talk and flirt with him,
Go on many diets to make myself slim.
Thinking he likes dumb girls, I failed all my tests,
Spend all my money on make-up, so he will be impressed.
He glances over at me, my heart falls to my feet,
Imagine us together, how that would be so sweet.
Hoping we would be together, living happily ever after,
Letting him fill my life with his joy and laughter.
Is this a fantasy, or is this real?
Wanting him to know how I feel.
When I see him, my palms get sweaty and hot
Does he love me, or love me not?

Charlie Kim Holmes (14)
Hesketh Fletcher High School, Atherton

Robert

(This is a true poem and it is dedicated to Robert Shaw.)

He was my friend
Until the end
A very good one too
I liked him a lot

The last thing
I said to him
So simple was
'See you on Hallowe'en'

He was my friend
Until the end
Or really
Until he died

He was too young
At 13 years old
I wish I could see
Him again

This was all
One year ago
But I feel
As if it was yesterday

We of course went
To the funeral
Though
It was a country away

Robert

I wish I could see him again.

Abe Treumann (12)
Marden Bridge Middle School, Whitley Bay

Daily Routine

Monday I wake up still half asleep
I eat my breakfast not making a peep
I rush out the house trying not to be late
The rest is boring, so I'll skip to the next date

Tuesday, I wake up bright and early
My hair is mad and very curly
I walk to school very slowly
I have my dinner, it's ravioli

Wednesday, I stumble out of bed
Then I stand up and bang my head
I run around trying to find my bag
My mam is sitting there reading her mag

Thursday, I can't wait to get up
My mam has coffee in her coffee cup
I watch TV and then go out
I see lots of people out and about

Friday I wake up very happy
But my bones feel very playful
Only one more day until the weekend
I am smiling, not going round the bend

Saturday, I lie in and relax
My dad has to pay the tax
I play my football and score a goal
I have some soup in a bowl

Sunday, I sleep until midday
I watch videos and I play
I wear my pyjamas all day long
I look for biscuits but there are none.

Sarah MacLeod (12)
Marden Bridge Middle School, Whitley Bay

My Mum

A mazing mother,
B rave other,
C lever thinker,
D aydreaming sleeper,
E ndless talker,
F antastic worker,
G ood tender,
H appy lover,
I ncorrect over,
J umping speaker,
K ind prancer,
L ovely maker,
M essy baker,
N ifty speaker,
O ink thrasher,
P oor dancer,
Q uiet seeker,
R idiculous player,
S ilent reader,
T errible diver,
U niversity skiver,
V icious scorer,
W itty mother,
X -ray hater,
Y ellow's powder,
Z ebra crowder.

Josh Oxley (12)
Marden Bridge Middle School, Whitley Bay

Frowning Man

There was a man
Who lived in town
He always had a funny frown
It made me laugh, it made me cry,
Until the day I die.

Jack White (13)
Marden Bridge Middle School, Whitley Bay

Christmas Presents

It's Christmas today
I feel so excited inside
Deep down in my stomach
I've got butterflies.
Will I get what I want -
Or will I get some socks?
I can't make my mind up
What's in that black box?

Underneath the big tree
It laughs and taunts
To rip it open now
Before my parents come down
I open up the curtains
Filling the room with light
As I peer out the frosted window
The garden is snowy and white.

I can hear footsteps upstairs
My parents are coming down
They look tired and sleepy
Both in dressing gowns.
All sat on the sofa
Mum, Dad and me
I tear open the black box
Oh my gosh, it's a PlayStation 3!

Jake Wilson (13)
Marden Bridge Middle School, Whitley Bay

Love Me?

Do you love me?
Say you do
Because I love you
Do you love me?
Please say you do
I love you
Please say I do.

Lewis Boyle (12)
Marden Bridge Middle School, Whitley Bay

Barmy Ben

Barmy Ben woke up and saw a hasty hen
So he ran, ran, ran to tell other men.
As he ran, ran, ran a colourful cow leapt in front of him
So Barmy Ben jumped, jumped, jumped over the colourful cow.
The colourful cow hit the hasty hen,
The hasty hen hit the colourful cow
So the colourful cow mooed at the hasty hen.
Barmy Ben booed at the colourful, now angry cow
So the colourful, now angry cow,
Clucked at Barmy Ben and the hasty hen
So the hasty hen mooed at the colourful, now angry cow.
The colourful, now angry cow squirted milk at the hasty hen
So the hasty hen threw an egg at the colourful, now eggy cow.
Barmy Ben shouted, 'Fight, fight, fight,' while he ran, ran, ran home.
While running, running, running home, he passed a mad monkey
Throwing bananas at a stealthful squirrel
Who was throwing acorns at the mad monkey.
The stealthful squirrel stealthily stole the monkey's bananas
So the monkey started to cry.
Barmy Ben gave the mad now crying monkey
The bananas from his packed lunch.
The now not crying mad monkey leapt, leapt, leapt with joy.
Barmy Ben laughed, laughed, laughed as he ran, ran, ran hastily home.

James Brookes (12)
Marden Bridge Middle School, Whitley Bay

Winter's Night

The icy breeze is like a spear,
The wind is howling out in fear.

The snow is covering the ground,
The night is silent, there's no sound.

The moon is shining in the dark blue sky,
Not a single person goes by.

This is what it's always like,
On a frosty winter's night.

Amy McCartney (12)
Marden Bridge Middle School, Whitley Bay

Socks And Fish

I went to the cinema
And milked a cow,
Tickled a pig,
I need cheese now,
So I flew to the moon
And I don't know how,
Made a rainbow,
Out of stuff.

I went to the dentist
And bought an eye,
Mine is glass,
Don't ask me why,
I went to JJB
And stole a fly,
I tickled it pink
And it died.

My mam tore her shirt,
Turned into Superman,
She said, 'Clean that dirt!'
So I walked into a wall
And bought a suitcase.

Hilly Hannam (12)
Marden Bridge Middle School, Whitley Bay

What A Goal!

Score a goal
The stadium rocks
Football captain
The whistle blows
Football boots
Weaving past the players
Unfair tackle
Red card shows
The free kick scores
The fans explode.

Jordan Robson (12)
Marden Bridge Middle School, Whitley Bay

Just Me And You

I hear my heartbeat in my head.
No more tears I need to shed.
You grin at me, I smile back too.
Alone, just me and you.

We walk along the moonlit beach.
All our sadness out of reach.
You hold onto my hand, stuck like glue.
Alone, just me and you.

The ocean is lapping at our feet.
How long I've waited for us to meet.
Your eyes dazzle me, the most deepest dark blue.
Alone, just me and you.

Now that the moon is bouncing off the sea.
I wonder why you would ever choose me.
I will never know, I just won't have a clue.
Alone, just me and you.

Your arm around my shoulders, you slow our pace.
You pull me close, now face to face.
Then you're gone, this feeling's new.
Alone, just me, not you.

Jemima Heasman (12)
Marden Bridge Middle School, Whitley Bay

My Days!

Gilagosh, Gilagish, there goes Jimmy he had a fish,
Put it on my dish,
My pants are tight, there goes the light,
The party's started, who just farted?
My make-up's smush, but that's all crush,
I had a talk, went for a walk.
Up on cloud nine, have you seen that pine?
What's the time? I need a lime.
Am going to bed, 'ave been fed!

Casey Lee Grieveson (12)
Marden Bridge Middle School, Whitley Bay

My Mother

Mother, I love you,
No matter what I say.
You mean the world to me,
No matter what I do.
When you are poorly, stressed or tired,
I'm here for you, just look and see.
Those days when I'm feeling down,
You're always there to comfort me.
I'll come to you with every problem,
Because you understand me.
And those terrible days, when you're away,
I always wish you were back, sitting there beside me.
Sometimes I say things I don't mean,
It doesn't mean I don't love you.
You are my mum, and nobody can replace you.
I love you so much, that if you went,
I don't know how I would cope.
Mum, you've done well,
For all you've been through.
Mum, I love you,
And I know you love me too.

Jessica Dix (13)
Marden Bridge Middle School, Whitley Bay

My Old Home

I miss my home
Back in Latvia
I miss my grandma
And my friends
I miss the weather
Which is snowy
And gets so hot in summertime
I miss the shops
And all the fun
I used to have
With my old friends.

Paul Lastockins (12)
Marden Bridge Middle School, Whitley Bay

My Friend Is?

Tan tights forgetter
Jet setter
Cookie buyer
Smiling liar
Mascara wearer
Presents bearer
Distance walker
Quick talker
Shaun hater
Clothes rater
Penguin painter
Fake fainter
Rubbish sailor
Blackmailer
Party lover
Run-for-cover
Teatree user
Chicken loser
Decent reader
Born leader.

Phoebe Watson (12)
Marden Bridge Middle School, Whitley Bay

Hunted

He is faster than a Ferrari.
He is an expert hunter.
His body requires lots of water.

As he sprints through the jungle
Searching for his prey
What does he find?

His leg is caught in a trap.
He has seconds before his life ends.
This is what has happened to most of his kind.

For he is a white tiger.
What has he done to deserve this?

Stephen Vose (12)
Marden Bridge Middle School, Whitley Bay

My Brother

Long sleeper
Slow walker
Quick runner
Quiet talker
Football player
Big liar
Smelly farter
Brother hater
Money spender
Money robber
Junk eater
Cool cooker
Teeth rotter
Good driver
No lover
Hard scarer
Injection hater
Great worker
Bad dancer
Quick reader.

Joseph Auchterlonie (12)
Marden Bridge Middle School, Whitley Bay

Love

It is mysterious,
It is fun,
When you know who it is,
The spark is never gone,
Sometimes it's tempered,
Sometimes it's messed,
But when you wake up
You always feel the best,
Love is always ace,
Love has its own pace,
It will appear,
Have no fear.

Thomas McDonough (12)
Marden Bridge Middle School, Whitley Bay

My Friends!

They make you happy when you're sad,
We're small and tall, we have it all,
We laugh at the bad times and the good,
The spirit of the group never dies!

They make you better when you're bad,
A simple smile will drive you mad,
We'll wait together in the good and the bad,
The spirit of the group never dies!

We're the petal of a flower so delicate and soft,
Sometimes rough, more often than not,
We are a jigsaw only complete with every piece,
The spirit of the group never dies!

We together are the chapters of a book,
So different yet the same,
Together we complete the flower,
Every petal in its own way,
The spirit of the group never dies!

Chelsea Byrne (12)
Marden Bridge Middle School, Whitley Bay

A Friend

A friend is like a flower,
A rose to be exact,
Bright they bloom,
Like a shiny spoon,
Or maybe a friend is like a brand new gate,
That never comes unlatched.
A friend is like a handcuff,
Which too never comes unlatched,
Unless you turn the wrong key,
Which makes it hard again to be attached.
A friend is like an owl,
Both beautiful and wise,
Or perhaps a friend is like a ghost,
Whose spirit never dies!

Bridie Munro (12)
Marden Bridge Middle School, Whitley Bay

Mad Granny

Knocking on the window,
Banging on the wall,
My granny runs round rabid,
After her long-distance fall.

Knocking on the window,
Banging on the wall,
My granny tries to use the phone,
For her monthly prank call.

Knocking on the window,
Banging on the wall.
My granny runs around screaming
While sprinting down the hall.

Knocking on the window,
Banging on the wall,
My granny finally stopped,
When my mother threw a ball.

James Wilson (12)
Marden Bridge Middle School, Whitley Bay

Random

I went to my friend's
And milked a cat.
I went to the moon
And bought a mat.
I went to the cinema
And watered a hat.
I went to the farm
And turned into a bat.
I went to school
And saw a blue rat.
I fed it bananas
Till it grew very fat.
I saw a fly wearing a tutu,
Do you believe all that?
Really, do you?

Amy Wilson (13)
Marden Bridge Middle School, Whitley Bay

My Dad

Big snorer,
Bad borer,
Funny cooker,
Big drooper,
Hilarious dancer,
Big prancer,
Class runner,
Mint stunner,
Funny joker,
Big boaster,
Big hugger,
Mother lover,
Messy writer,
Funny fighter,
Computer master,
Baking disaster.

Noi Jenkinson (12)
Marden Bridge Middle School, Whitley Bay

My Crazy, Random Nonsense Poem!

I went to the shops
And bought a lamp post,
I went to school and the teacher exploded,
I saw a dinosaur praying at church,
I went to the moon
And saw a platypus,
I asked what it was doing all the way up there,
It said, 'I don't know, but it's tip top my dear.'
I flew to the sun and met an alien,
I roasted marshmallows
And he said he was called Jim.
I went to my friend's to see what she was up too,
When I got there, she was having a tea party with a cuckoo,
I went back to bed at the end of my day,
I said, 'That was random and crazy,
Oh look over there, it's a daisy!'

Rebecca Cross (12)
Marden Bridge Middle School, Whitley Bay

Romeo And Juliet

Romeo
Romeo watching you walk away
My mind went astray
Watching, me Juliet
I quietly silently wept
And every time my eyes leaked blue
It was from always thinking of you

Juliet
Juliet I hate it when I leave
As I walk through your garden
And all the woodland trees
But one day soon
In the light of the day
We'll run away
Staying forever and always together.

Sarah Elkin (12)
Marden Bridge Middle School, Whitley Bay

Newcastle FC

N ew manager every season
E verlasting hope for a last minute goal
W aiting on the edge of seats
C hanting out the names of goal scorers
A sking questions of the ref
S tarting to get worried of relegation
T ogether we are one as a team
L oyal to our roots as we always have been
E ven though, loving our team

F orever waiting for a cup
C hanging never from black and white.

Daniel Atkin (12)
Marden Bridge Middle School, Whitley Bay

Skateboarding

Skateboarding is my hobby
That I love most of all.
Skating hurts a lot
Especially when you fall.
Skating parks
Trucks make marks.
Tricks up ramps
Are very hard
But most of all
I have fun
As I skate in the sun.

Andrew Rigg (12)
Marden Bridge Middle School, Whitley Bay

Me!

My hair is a stack of hay in the morning.
My eyes are the sea all whirled up in a ball.
In badminton I am blind as a bat.
My mind is a constantly used computer.
Sharp knives are my nails.
My ears are as small as a mini digestive.
My skin is the colour of a freshly picked apple.
My cheeks are cherry tomatoes.

Hannah Gilroy (13)
Marden Bridge Middle School, Whitley Bay

A Snake

He looks so big and scary
As he slithers on the sand
His skin is slimy and scaly
As he moves across the land
His eyes look like marbles
He's like a monster in the dark
If you see him, you'd better run.

Aaron Goldwater (12)
Marden Bridge Middle School, Whitley Bay

I've Never Met A Shark Before

I've never met a shark before
Never in my life.
But I love how it glides
And moves from side to side.
He has so many teeth
He lives beneath the reef.
I've never met a shark before
Never in my life.

Andy Tweedy (12)
Marden Bridge Middle School, Whitley Bay

A Crocodile

He looks scary
Looks mean and cruel
He has sharp teeth
And sharp nails too
He reminds me of a dinosaur
With his big powerful jaws
A crocodile, that's what you are.

Raymond Tough (12)
Marden Bridge Middle School, Whitley Bay

I Hate My Life

I hate my life
A tragedy has happened
I am in shock
Everyone in my family is crying
I wish the world would stop and let me off
I can't believe it
I've just lost my dad.

Daniel David Walker (12)
Marden Bridge Middle School, Whitley Bay

Friendship

Friends are great,
You get to play out,
Friendship is commitment,
It doesn't feel like that,
It feels like a sister or brother,
Friends are gold,
Forever when you're old.

Connor Murray (12)
Marden Bridge Middle School, Whitley Bay

I Am

I am the brain
That has to remain
Asleep, crying away,
I should say.

She asks the question,
It is for me,
But not yet,
I am not the teacher's pet.

My nerves start to tingle,
Is this my time to mingle?
Please be cool,
Or I will walk away from school.

This is a worry
That is like a hot curry,
Burning me away.
I shoot my hand up,
And I'm okay!

This is not a worry,
I am still alive,
Actually, I made quite a show!
My friend put down that cigarette,
And no one has to fret.

Meg Jameson-Allen (11)
Ripon Grammar School, Ripon

Dear Dad

When you wake up in the morning,
And go to sleep at night.
Remember I'm here,
Don't feel fright.

When you gather your kit,
Or grasp your gun,
Know that you're loved,
Dad, brother, son.

When you think of the memories,
That we've shared before,
Look to the future,
Know that there'll be more.

When you fire your weapon,
See the dead.
You're doing the right thing,
Keep that in your head.

When you're packed to leave,
On your way back.
Look forward to life,
Not being under attack.

When you see us,
And we hold you tight,
We'll smile at each other,
Filled with such delight.

When you're stood next to me,
I'm glad that you're here,
By the end of this poem,
You'll probably shed a tear.

I love you so much
As you already know.
You'll leave again sometime,
I don't want you to go!

Shannon Millar (12)
Ripon Grammar School, Ripon

Sticks And Stones Hurt My Bones

I run down the alley, pursuers on my tail,
As I wonder whether their persistence will ever fail.
Panting and crying, calling for a friend,
Just cos they think being a geek ain't a trend.
Suddenly I slip, I scramble to the floor,
Attempting to unearth that imaginary trap door.
Their presence booming, here to end it for me,
Just being a geek caused this ending to be!

Then they arrive . . .

They put me against the wall,
Each one smiling and standing tall.
I want them to hit me and end it here,
An unbearable childhood - but when I die,
Bet the murderers will cheer.
I can't fight or stand up for myself,
No bodyguard or protection even with all my family's wealth.
They hit me once and repeat it again,
I know it won't end, but to die at the age of ten!
A horrible fate as I dearly pray,
If only God could help me on this horrific day.

They pick up the rock and smash my face,
Death and bleakness my unrivalled fate.
I watch and stare, mouth o-shaped,
Their minds pure evil, as if all happiness has escaped.
I'm sorry God for all my sins
And because of this I've had no breaks or wins,
But Heaven or Hell, which will it be?
It doesn't matter, my life is about to begin.
Whether upset or happy the story is set
Simply being a geek has caused my *death*.

Edward Lyons (11)
Ripon Grammar School, Ripon

Untitled

Charity week begins,
And we're all having fun,
Teachers humiliating themselves,
First years selling buns.

Guess the teddy bear,
And raffles in the hall,
How many sweets in a jar?
Stuff selling from a stall.

Some are going on a trip,
Whilst others go to school,
They're buying tickets for the
Smiths' concert in the hall.

The week is almost over,
It's all gone by so fast,
But all that really matters,
Is the ruined lives that go past.

Whilst we're all having fun,
Laughing all day,
Another child over there,
Slowly passes away.

So let's take time,
To think about,
The pain they're going through,
All the children over there,
Dying just for you.

Issy Gould (11)
Ripon Grammar School, Ripon

Frog - Haiku

Small, gleaming, green frog,
Sitting on a lily pad,
Plop, into the pond.

Megan Aspinall (16)
Ripon Grammar School, Ripon

Mortal

The first tick of new life
Sebreeta I ask
And the flight begins with the ease of that laugh
Sebreeta through jungles, by portals and flying
The minutes too repetitive and new to be dying
See the seconds fall back and collide
Be the one who always delves inside
Ta-ta tootles, whoopee and hooray!
Until stuck and fade . . .
The first dong of the hour
Seeing the breath of the space that now teeters
A backwards glance at the (unretrievable) light?
To ask thyself . . . thou Lord has blessed thy with thy life?
The second hour passes
The springing tick has gone?
Sebreeta still present though cold to the touch
Midnight sounds and
A twin of the others same years that she shares
The clone-like tomorrow throwing minutes to dust
Now a structure that must do to survive?
And the hand now forcing the (flying?)
An hour indeed of a death is upon her?
When we must be thrown forward to chill
As is the truth of these lost rotations
In rediscovering those feelings of youth?
The old choice, so be it.
Exist.

Jessica Burgess (16)
Ripon Grammar School, Ripon

Winter - Haiku

Snow covers the fields
Crystal flakes fall on the ground
Winter has arrived.

Emma Beaumont (11)
Ripon Grammar School, Ripon

Saved By The Bell

Mechanics swirl round and round,
To make that ever-so-special sound.
A rhythm, a beat, a clickety click.
That well-known constant tick-tock-tick.
I watch the second hand fly by,
Waiting for the time when I,
Shall hear the shrill bell loud and clear,
Signalling crowds of youths to appear.
Bright orange coaches do await,
But not for those who come too late!
To grunt and groan themselves away,
And deliver us like mail each day.
Alas, not yet, lessons still are here!
And what's that whisper in my ear?
Oh no! A question I've been asked!
My peaceful daydreaming unmasked!
I feel my face turn cherry red,
I fiddle with a small loose thread
What did she say? I do not know!
Oh drat my thoughts, oh no! Oh no!
What shall I do? I haven't a clue!
Say something right out of the blue?
Wait, what's that sound I hear?
Which fills each and every hopeful ear?
How happy I am! For it's not a knell!
'Tis the end of the day!
I've been saved by the bell!

Megan Ruth Oakeley (13)
Ripon Grammar School, Ripon

Homework - Haiku

It squats there waiting,
As daunting as a mountain
The end, of spare time.

Ashley Lowe (16)
Ripon Grammar School, Ripon

So Many Issues

I'm meant to write a poem,
And yet I can't decide
What to say, what to admit,
So many things I have to confide.

There's the issue of war,
So many people dead.
Or there are people being bullied,
Saying words that can't be said.

There's the issue of pollution,
Doing things without a care,
Or the fact that I'm worried
About the things I wear.

The fact that so many people
Don't have enough food,
Or the comments I hear,
That are just plain rude.

The fact that animals I love
May become extinct,
Because we do selfish things,
As we just don't think.

So many issues,
So much that's wrong,
Why don't we see things coming?
Why do we wait so long?

Ashleigh Messenger (12)
Ripon Grammar School, Ripon

Guitar - Haiku

I play the guitar,
Strum, strum, strum, strum, steel string strum.
Oh you twelve bar blues.

Zack Duffy (11)
Ripon Grammar School, Ripon

The Consequences Of War!

What do you think when someone says the word *war*
Maybe the words that might come into your head
are *blood* and *gore*.
When the army manages to win a prestigious battle,
it opens a new door
But obviously only for the country that you're fighting for.

As fellow soldiers fall thick and fast
You might start looking back to the past
When these soldiers used to be your friends
The ones that led you through every corner and bend.

Some day it will be over,
And we'll look towards the white cliffs of Dover
In one or more losing countries will mourn
But in the winning country a new start will dawn.

War destroys everyone and we know it
As countries are defeated bit by bit
People will be killed and kill
But war carries on . . . still.

Will the world ever be full of love?
Even when push comes to shove
We'll always go through the highs and the lows,
But as always, the wind always will blow . . .

Michael Hasan (12)
Ripon Grammar School, Ripon

Home Is . . .

Home is where the thick, lush grass grows beneath the juicy soil
Home is my own part of this world
My own chunk of land, my rules.
Purple tastes like pure evil, anger, revenge.
Red sounds painful like when I hear
The screaming voices of pain in children.
Blue sounds like the sea whispering
'Hush, hush,' whenever we meet.

Maddie Botros (12)
Ripon Grammar School, Ripon

Brainstorm

Head spinning starting to explode,
Info whizzing into hyperdrive mode,

Is my homework done yet?
Am I becoming a teacher's pet?
Am I too fat, too tall, too skinny,
Or am I just being silly?

What if my friends desert me?
Where at lunchtime would I be?
Behind the shed smoking cigarettes
Or in the art room watching paint set?

What if global warming gets worse?
Would we get in a rocket and jet off first?
Or would I be stuck on Earth
Trapped with the polar ice caps which got off worse?
What would happen if I got an F?
Then school turns into one big, big mess!

All these worries seem like a lot
However at home I've got . . .
A solid, amazing support system too,
Of family and friends, aunties and uncles!
All waiting to give me one whooping great cuddle!

Emma Hope (11)
Ripon Grammar School, Ripon

Midnight

M idnight is when the weeping willow twists and turns to take its prey.
 I n the moonlight the wolf stalks its prey.
D ipping and turning the hairy spider swoops to finish his web.
N ettles sway from side to side with the wind.
 I ncredibly the moonlight trickles in through the thick beech trees.
G ently the leaves start to fall to the soft, mossy ground.
H edgehogs sniffle around finding their midnight snack.
 T he dawn breaks, then everything goes quiet.

Will Andrew (11)
Ripon Grammar School, Ripon

Coping

He came home from his op today,
His crutches round both arms.
All sad and bad for us all to see,
But a shock, he was so calm.

He sat there struggling to get up.
I wondered what to do.
He shouted back in my face,
'I don't need help from you.'

How small and helpless would he feel,
Barely being able to walk,
How lucky he was to have family,
To them he could talk and talk.

Day by day his legs grew stronger,
Soon he was out playing football.
It was great to see him back to himself.
Still so very tall.

His second op is on its way,
How frightful it must be.
Who will be there by his side.
But his caring family.

Zoë Umpleby (12)
Ripon Grammar School, Ripon

If I Ruled The World . . .

If I ruled the world.
There would be no weapons or wars.

If I ruled the world,
Everyone would be equal and we would share the world's resources.

If I ruled the world,
We would try to cure all disease and care for everyone.

But I don't rule the world,
We all rule the world,
And we can change the world by working together.

Alannah Mae Mansfield (12)
Ripon Grammar School, Ripon

You Are . . .

You are my fire on the coldest nights,
You are a star that shines so bright,
You are the one that lightens my life,
You are . . .

You are the warmth that glows in me,
You are something wonderful which fills me with glee,
You are the largest gem you'll ever see,
You are . . .

You are my only, my one true love,
You are like a bright white dove.
You are an angel from the heavens above,
You are . . .

You are like crystals and barrels of treasure,
You are the person that fills me with pleasure,
You are the one I'd replace for leisure,
You are . . .

You are as beautiful as the sun when it rises,
You are a wonder that's full of surprises,
You are the one I'd send red roses,
You are . . .

Rebecca Boarman (11)
Ripon Grammar School, Ripon

Why?

Why do I wonder why the world goes round?
Why do I wonder why the grass is green?
Why do I wonder what makes me upset?
And why I just wept and wept.
Why do I wonder why we're all jealous and greedy?
Why do I wonder why there is so much crime?
Why people break out, and not do their time?
People say it's weird to wonder why,
But take it or leave it,
Because that is I.

Madeleine Marston (11)
Ripon Grammar School, Ripon

My Dad

My dad is:

A football fan,
Family man.
Computer geek,
Not very sleek.
Bald head,
Stays in bed.

Brain box,
No sort of fox.
Was in army.
Quite barmy.
Drives a car,
Likes the bar.

Sometimes flies,
Tells no lies.
Eats curry,
Not like Andy Murray.
Sort of chubby,
My mum's hubby.

That's my dad!

Lauren Bradwell (11)
Ripon Grammar School, Ripon

Feathery Friends

Pecking at the worms and flying in the sky,
With majestic wings away they fly,
Up, up, up to a puffy white cloud,
Puffing out their chest, standing tall and proud.
They build their homes in a labyrinth of leaves,
Pulling it together with struggles and heaves,
Twigs, branches, rocks, anything they can find,
Putting it together with a weave and a wind.
Now they have a home for all year round,
I think I'll be safe as long as it's not found.

Matthew Cotton (11)
Ripon Grammar School, Ripon

Teased Tears

Strong in soul,
Fierce in heart,
Brown hair, blue eyes,
Just for a start.
There are many qualities
That make the person I call 'Me'.

But of all these things, oh why, oh why
Why does teasing make me cry?

Of all the things to tear my eyes,
Blear my eyes,
Make good thoughts hide,
Why does teasing make me cry?

A single name can make me shiver,
My blood run cold, my anger quiver.
My ire's fires spit and burn,
'Cause someone called me 'useless cur!'
Of all the things to make my mouth dry,
My brain fry,
My patience try,
Why does teasing make me cry?

Rebekah Vanzo (13)
Ripon Grammar School, Ripon

Stop

You say, 'They'll just get bored, they'll go away,'
But you don't have to hear it every day
You say, 'It's only words, not sticks, nor stones,'
So surely words won't break my bones?

You say you're 'Here to help.'
But then you say to 'Help yourself.'
Who will help, right here, right now.
Who will pick me up when I am down?

I tell them to stop but they don't care.
Why me? It's so unfair.

Elleanor Lamb (11)
Ripon Grammar School, Ripon

Caring For Material

It's hard to care for some,
Sometimes I think I care too much.
For him, for her, them.
I can't care enough. Do I?
Caring about myself,
Or just my reputation.
Putting on fashionable clothes
And too much make up.
High street brands
I am a brand
Or I have been branded
Not me, no not me.
Wanting so much more, getting just less.
Material girl with friends that care
About calories, figures, hair
Sometimes, it's just not enough.
I feel trapped inside this fake shell.
Just me isn't enough for you is it?
I can be me
But not now, not yet.
When the time's right, I'll come out again.

Sophie Charlton (12)
Ripon Grammar School, Ripon

Unique

There's only one of me,
And there's only one of you.
I am unique and you are too.

We are all very special in our own little way,
Making different choices, every single day.

I'm an individual, one of a kind,
Using my own independent mind.

Wherever we are,
Whatever we do,
I am unique and you are too.

Imogen Oakes (11)
Ripon Grammar School, Ripon

My Feelings For The Environment

I look at the Earth from Nature's point of view
But look at all the pollution too
With the cavemen it was fair
No pollution so nature did not need to care
It was the same with the kings and the queen
But then we came along, big and mean
Ever heard of global warming?
What a place Earth is forming
From a globe to a throbbing wreck
With pollution and steam up to our neck
Well I say let's save our land
Let us lend a helping hand
Do not sit!
Do not wait!
In this world do not hate
There is still time
Do not fear
Do not despair
Do not shed a tear
Listen carefully to all who say
We can still change the fate of the Earth today.

Jack Burgess (12)
Ripon Grammar School, Ripon

Mysterious

M ystic lights surround the place with eagle eyes, glaring,
Y oung children race towards the place; staring
S himmering stars, come down and group, huddled together around,
T ranquil colours bulge and bound;
E verlasting sun beams on, only the face,
R ed eyes stare out at the wonderful chase,
I don't know what's happening; I don't know what to do,
O ut I reveal my face full of horrid slime and goo,
U tter disgrace spreads through the crowd,
S eeing my mysterious soul, I roar clear and loud . . .

Leanne Anderson (11)
Ripon Grammar School, Ripon

Heartbeat

Heartbeat
By my watch
It is time.

I taste autumn frost.
A vortex of swirling leaves surrounds us,
The harshness of the day pierces my bones.
I turn to you,
Am enveloped in your warmth.

Azure oceans
I could dive
Immerse myself
In those perfect lagoons.

Silence
The tick of two hearts,
Shallow soft whisper of my breath,
Anticipation.

Time stops,
Soft velvet lips.
Peal of drumming bells.

Eleanor Duffield (16)
Ripon Grammar School, Ripon

Nobody Like Family

I wear my mask in hard times.
Why let my emotions show?
Nobody really wants to know a person who is miserable.
I am a computer, wires dead.
Expressionless, tired, preserved in a spell.
A weathered stone, bruises numbed under ice,
Even a ripple of laughter can't escape my lips,
As I crumble, passing time
My pain stored away inside.
But my mask is only made of ice,
And so the sun will thaw -
Light will shine, break through the cracks,
With the heat warming my core
Here, the fear lacks
For how can anyone resist the joy a younger sibling gives?
They're innocent, small and filled with glee
For love and attention they're in need
They're the ones my world goes around,
And break the mask that's had me bound.
I'm still me, but with a different face.

Aimee Rutherford (12)
Ripon Grammar School, Ripon

Mum And Me

We ran together Mum and me.
Along the stretch of sand and sea.
The water rushes up the beach.
Hidden are the rocks beneath.
The sun rays' warmth upon my back;
As we chase along this golden track.
The sand like tiny grains of rice.
The waves roll back in a trice.
The wind so playful with my hair.
Time slips by without a care.
A better time I can't dream,
As now I lick a toffee ice cream.

Victoria Frost (11)
Ripon Grammar School, Ripon

What Can We Do?

It's terrible, terrible, what should I do?
We're running out of money
What about you?
My family are getting hungry
Nothing left to eat
It's getting so bad!
Us children don't get treats!
The money crisis has hit us
That is what's wrong
We could all be in trouble
There's not very long!
Soon they'll have to close the shops
Because no one's going there.
I don't know how to solve it
There is no one who cares!
So how can we solve it?
What can we do?
It's getting worse.
But there's nothing we can do!

Kate Grime (11)
Ripon Grammar School, Ripon

The Bully

Little Miss Popular
Pretends you're her friend
Everyone likes her
But she drives you up the bend.

Her vicious words
Come out like a knife
Intended for you
It ruins your life.

The words they stay with you
They are never forgotten
They are always in your mind
Tied up like cotton.

Lucy Chapman (12)
Ripon Grammar School, Ripon

Stop!

My whole life is passing before me,
Why must we rush them so?
What happened today is just a memory,
And it is hard to let go.
Stop!
Why must we cry?
And feel emotions?
Does anyone really know?
What is the point of living with no ambition?
Stop!
I feel lost in a room with a lock and no key.
Everything is moving with such haste,
It is as if I am trapped for eternity
Yesterday has gone without a trace.
Stop!
So many questions I have yet to ask,
But why can't we all just slow down?
Just notice the world, please, at last.
For a moment please stop and look around.

Jess Alice Butterell (13)
Ripon Grammar School, Ripon

Loved Ones

They always care
They always share
They are always near
They are always so dear
They are always loved
They are always close, but never shoved
They are always there

But then they're gone, never to be back
They're still there, deep down and up above.
Watching over, but it'll never be enough
They're gone; never to be back
Life isn't always fair.

Heather Laws (13)
Ripon Grammar School, Ripon

No One

I stand alone,
The wind in my hair but no life by my side.
I sit on the bench,
They said they'd be here, they lied.
I lie on my bed,
My tears for company for no friends are there.

I change schools,
Not many hopes for the new start.
I say hello,
I get a smile and the name of Mark.
I walk home smiling,
My first good day of school.

My third year,
'His' and 'Hellos' from all sides.
I sit on the bench,
They are here, they were right.
I lie on my bed,
My good friends for company, no more need for tears.

Sam Cooper (11)
Ripon Grammar School, Ripon

War, It Can't Go On

Bullets whizzing, buildings falling
When will it end?
There's no need for it, let peace and love take our heart,
No hatred and anger, don't let them take you
People dying, bombs falling,
Stop it or it could be you who's there.
See what they go through, it's the highway to Hell,
Only you can stop it.
Don't let people suffer.
Think of love, put down your weapons and be friends
We don't want wars, millions of deaths,
Have love and passion for your fellow man.

Jamie Bowker (12)
Ripon Grammar School, Ripon

The Tree

A soul cannot be taken, as a tree cannot move.
The withered oak sitting there,
Lost its life when it is clear.
They came with bark set ablaze,
From those they killed another day.
They brought creatures with razor teeth,
That growled when they command.
The roaring beasts set their work
By biting through the wooden flesh.
They burned the roots of the oak
And skilled its leafy friends.
They left, burning the oak
But new trees will grow and consume them
For hidden, shrouded,
Within the vines and thorns and brambles,
Lies a soul
The living hope.
The forest.

Theo Lumsden (11)
Ripon Grammar School, Ripon

The Class

I sit here all alone,
With the class blurting in my ear,
The teacher blends into the board,
With her sharp finger pointing right at me,
Everyone turns around like a bolt of lightning,
I look up at the board,
But it just looks back at me,
The words just seem to float off,
Off into their own world,
But then she comes,
She comes and helps me,
She helps me blend in,
And the bubble just pops . . .
I'm back again.

Jessica Bryden (12)
Ripon Grammar School, Ripon

6.30am, Sept 4th Rap

Today I start at grammar and I'm scared I'll need a wiz,
Cos I don't know where the nearest toilet is.
I've got ma grammar blazer and my brass buttons
And those brass buttons I didn't get 'em from Duttons
In fact they cost the oldies six whole quid,
And that reminds me - for tea I'm havin' squid.
I've got ma new bus pass that's in its little holder
That's in my briefcase, that's got a little folder.
The granmar's got a swimming pool and I'm so excited
And I'm really glad that I'm not short-sighted.
I've got ma swimmin' kit and ma new backpack
That's got ma Nike rugby boots in a plastic bag.
I've got ma new school shoes ready with ma sox
And ma new scarf and ma locker lock
Ah think I got everythin' except my rugger kit,
But I better pack it quick and really hop it.
I better get the bus fast and show the man ma pass
And make him put his foot down or I'll be late for class.

Richard Langdale (12)
Ripon Grammar School, Ripon

Pushing And Pulling

Terrible images, nightmares among.
Horrible images, being hit by gongs.
In this world of horrible dreams,
I'm pretty scared of 'spilling the beans'.
When will it end?
If it will at all
Listen, listen, I hear them coming!
Listen to them, them talking, more like mulling
Everlasting, this pulling and pushing.
Never ending, new dark thoughts seeping through my mind.
Does this mean it never ends?
No it does not, if people listen.
Only when people know
We can pull through when those dark thoughts go.

Tom Sladen (11)
Ripon Grammar School, Ripon

Beating Up The Bully

I will fight the searing pain
I will not let him flush me down the drain,
One day I will get him back
Then he'll finally feel the crack.

I go home at night creating my plan
Maybe I should use a frying pan
Then *he* will feel the searing pain
And *I* will flush him down the drain.

Then he'll go home with a hurt frown
Even though his hair is brown
He sees his parents big and butch
They don't seem to understand much.

He'll cry himself to sleep at night
With the thought of me, the evil fright
Whether he'll come back at me
I must tell you it's a mystery.

Max Crompton (12)
Ripon Grammar School, Ripon

Instructions, Restrictions

Instructions, instructions,
What do they mean?
Do this! Do that!
Restricting a dream.
We all have desires,
But instructions start fires,
Burning our free will unseen.
Sometimes we have to do things we don't like.
But it's often worth it to make things work out right.
Instructions, instructions,
Often for our benefit,
But some will not follow them just for the fun of it.
It's good to have fun and to be a young soul rebel
But you've got to restrict yourself,
And decide which way to throw your pebble.

Nathan Atkinson (13)
Ripon Grammar School, Ripon

Charity Week

Lots of cake, lots of chocolate, lots of fun,
Late for classes,
Stalls at break,
No one on time.

Battle of the bands,
The Smiths in concert,
World record attempt,
The panel show.

Never dull, always bright,
Stuffing our faces with cookies day in, day out,
Non-uniform day,
To our delight.

Just one week.
All money for War Child,
Lots of money just for them,
And we all helped!

Anna Durkin (11)
Ripon Grammar School, Ripon

I Am It

I am it,
I am the thing that you fear,
I could be a slug,
But I could be your tear,
Only you know what I am,
For I am your nightmare,
I am the creaky floorboard,
I am the flickering light,
Whatever I am
I will give you a fright,
So,
If you are in the dark,
Don't say I didn't warn you,
When I have crushed you with
Fear.

Kimberley Hall (11)
Ripon Grammar School, Ripon

War

Pain and destruction,
Flying limbs all around,
Grenades and missiles,
Hit the ground.

Dirt and sweat
Digging in the ground
Shifting soil with your spade,
And on your right is the mound.

The mound of men,
Who have risked their lives for their country,
Yet who fight for nothing,
What was the point?

So many people dead,
As we all bow our head,
To remember the soldiers,
Who died . . . for nothing.

Lewis Bartlem (11)
Ripon Grammar School, Ripon

Fighting And War

F ighting and war, annoys me to the core,
I feel them scared, the cold, the pain,
'G o away,' I hear them shout, pointing to the door,
H itting them and their children with a big metal chain,
T highs aching, backs bleeding,
I nside their hearts are melting,
N arrow doors knocked down, behind women kneading,
G ashes showing from their beating.

A ll day and night,
N ever see a different sight,
D ying like this isn't right.

W eight decreasing fast,
A ll they can hear is a blast,
R avenous people, leaving at last.

Evie Don (12)
Ripon Grammar School, Ripon

The Christmas Boxes

I see the truck, coming up the road.
Children in ragged clothes,
Coming rushing out of their mud houses,
Their dark, dirty faces turning ecstatic,
The time has come.
Rushing up to the truck, lost in the crowd,
The doors open and white men step out.
My people, overawed, not used to that pale tone of skin
Then come the boxes handed out to us,
Grabbing hands, reaching out,
The wrapping ripped off and joy is floating around
We see the toys and useful things,
Some of which have been unknown.
The white man hands one to me
And my heart soars in anticipation
As I carefully open the box and see all the treasures.
The best Christmas yet.

Shannon Groves (11)
Ripon Grammar School, Ripon

Sticks And Stones

Sticks and stones may break my bones
But words will never hurt me
This is not true, it cannot be,
For words can trap you
Can't you see?
For words are hurtful, dark as night
It's like being trapped, but with more bite
'I'm scared, I'm scared I can't get out.'
This box with walls made out of spite
Full of hatred, full of fear, I am my only friend, 'Oh dear!'
Although the words I'm hearing
Now have cut me off from friends
A couple of special words though
Could make this nightmare end.

Thomas Lonsdale (11)
Ripon Grammar School, Ripon

That Couple

His short, spiky hair
Why should she care?
They're in love
Free like a dove
They're not alone
They're in the zone
Together forever
Apart never ever.

Annabelle Ayliffe (12)
Ripon Grammar School, Ripon

It's Not Who I Am On The Outside But Who I Am On The Inside.

I walk into the room, it's filled with light.
People laughing and playing seem so bright.
I keep walking and walking as their heads all turn,
'Who is that girl?' someone said very stern.
I closed my eyes and wished and wished
Hoping the ground would swallow me up as a fish.
People were murmuring now, around the room,
I was red in the face like a sailor with sunburn.
My hands were shaking now, I felt really sick,
When can the bell go? As the clock went tick.
Soon a girl came up to me, quite shy she seemed,
And sat down beside me, soon enough she beamed.
She is now my friend you see she saw right through me
Because she knew it's not who you are on the outside
But who you are on the inside.

Sophie Reed (11)
Ripon Grammar School, Ripon

War . . .

I sat alone in my room
I waited for that great big boom
In the corner I would cry
On the floor my family would lie
I lie still, not moving a muscle
In the corner without a hustle.

In the sky far, far away above the clouds
Down below he could see the crowds
Drops his bombs looking proud
When he looks out onto the crowds
He sees death and damage.

In the hospital I would lie
Staring at the clear blue sky
Looking at my rusty brown bed
Next to me my father lay
'Get well soon,' my mother would say.

Nicola Terry (12)
Ripon Grammar School, Ripon

Bullying: The Figure Of Evil

I don't really have any friends,
When will my suffering end?
I really, really hate my life,
The bully's words feel like a knife,
Twisting into my poor broken heart,
One last punch and I'll fall apart.

But we can beat this evil figure,
Don't back down and fight with vigour,
Live your life with love and passion,
Just forget wealth and fashion,
It's not what's on the outside,
It's inside,
It's deeper
If we look deeper and all get on
Together we can beat bullying.

Bently Briggs (12)
Ripon Grammar School, Ripon

White-Out Rider

Ice crystals sparkle white in blue,
Deep snow, board carving through.
Skin tingling in cold air,
Wind rustling through my hair.
The boarder slides through powder and ice,
Carving through, slice by slice.

Chris Wallace (15)
Ripon Grammar School, Ripon

Alzheimer's

It dissolves her memory.
It wastes her away.
Forgetting what life is for,
It's the price she had to pay.

My emotions went all crazy,
When my grandma died last month.
It awoke me to the truth,
Like a long, hard punch.

There is no need for such a curse,
I wish they'd find a cure.
For I don't want another soul,
To lose life's memories so pure.
22,000 people,
Die from it every year.
The burden that ends people's lives,
Well that is very clear.

Constance Lumsdon (11)
Ripon Grammar School, Ripon

Why Do We Listen To Popular Music?

Why do we listen to popular music?
Do we all really like it?
Is it so good?
Or do we listen to it because others do?
Why do humans want to follow others,
Being led as if they are blind?
Do they want to be accepted?
Do they want to fit in?
Music, fashion, smoking, drugs . . .
Are they really so different?
Why walk when you can run?
Why aim low and not higher?
Why not achieve to your best?
Why be the same when you can be better?
Follow your dreams and aspirations,
You are unique . . . you can change our world forever.

Harry Yates (13)
Ripon Grammar School, Ripon

Always There

They'll never be too busy
They'll never be too tired
They'll never be too far away
To listen to what I have to say
They'll never interrupt me
Or cut me off to watch TV
They'll just sit there and listen
I feel they understand me
After I've moaned on and on
They know just what to do
They nuzzle my hand and look in my eyes
And make an adorable puffing sound
I wish people were more like them
They help me through bad days
They are Misty and Gemma
My little guinea pig babes.

Francesca Howe (13)
Ripon Grammar School, Ripon

Bullies Aren't Nice

Bullies aren't nice
In my eyes they are no bigger than the 'one' on a dice
Bullies aren't nice.
In my mind they are just a grain of rice
Bullies aren't nice
In my heart they are slippier than ice
Bullies aren't nice
In my head bullies very much entice
Bullies aren't nice
In every breath there's so much fear
You know, bullies are really not nice
But remember, there are people who can give advice
I'm sure you can assume they'll be nice
They will.
Because they're there to help cover the bill.
Just for you and anyone else who is suffering.

Regan Raffle (12)
Ripon Grammar School, Ripon

Best Friend Betrayal

I come to school for friendship
But really I see the ship sinking
I also see my friend winking
It means nothing, I already know
I can't believe my brain moved so slow
He hits on purpose but like a joke
I can already tell I'll get a choke
On the bus we sit at the back
He quickly gets off hiding my sack
I confront him the next day, he says he does not
I confront him again and so he fights
Here and there throwing punches and lunging
I stay still and talk while he tries to make me go plunging
I win with my soul, he wins with his body
'Friendship is whatever you can still betray - betrayal can only happen if you have friendship.'

James Douglas Hamilton (11)
Ripon Grammar School, Ripon

All Is Well . . .

Sweeping hair caught by the wind,
With an adorable curl on one side.
Sparkling eyes reflect through the glass, brown.
Goes through me. I see him.
Courageous, kind. An amazing guy.
Top button undone and shirt untucked,
Staggering, yet scruffy, standing in the crowd.
Dark blue blazer, ripped at the seams
Graffitied folders and defeated deadlines.
Fun, loud, lazy. Detention. Again.
Mud on his shoes, paint on his hands,
Presence of talent, absence of work.
Sitting on a table top, smile across his face,
Laughing at a friend's expense.
Scared, hopeless. Drowning in mistakes.
Saturday night, he might work hard,
But saving up for the next Friday night.
He wanders down the street, lights up. Drunk.
Friends at hand to guide the dummy home.
The trouble, the mess, the regrets, the future?
Where has the sense gone? The smile gone?
The charm, the joy, the love, the happiness? Gone.
Do I believe it will get better?
Do I have hope
Or do I accept him, the man I love? Still present.
Staring right through me. A teardrop.
It doesn't matter, because in the morning,
Once again,
He is well
And all is well.

Abigail Ward (14)
Ripon Grammar School, Ripon

The Way You Make Me Feel

I hear your name,
I see you in the corridor,
Butterflies fill my stomach,
I love to hear your laugh,
I love to see you smile,
Warmth fills my heart.

Every time you call I'm filled with joy,
I could sit and talk to you for hours.
Then comes this awkward silence that so many like to break,
But this kind is different.
It's the kind of silence you don't mind having around,
The kind when you realise,
The person you love is just a call away,
And he's there for you throughout each day.

When you stare into my eyes, it's a feeling I can't ignore,
When I am wrapped up in your arms, I feel safer than ever before.
I know that what I feel for you,
I never felt with anyone else.
Every time we're together, I'm overwhelmed with happiness,
I have no worries,
I feel no pain,
You take away my fears,
You let me shine again.

Words can't express how much I love you,
I hope you realise that my love for you is real.
With you, is where I want to be,
All I see in this world,
Is no one else but you and me.

Megan Lane (16)
Ripon Grammar School, Ripon

Couldn't Be Bothered

Couldn't be bothered at school
Couldn't be bothered to work
Couldn't be bothered to concentrate

They said to me, 'Focus, boy.'
They put up with my behaviour
They tried to help me out
They said, 'You'll fail,' I took no notice

Can't go to study at university
Can't afford to buy a house
Can't find a job
Can't get any cash

I thought life would be easy
I thought life would be fun
Not listening at school
Was the worst thing I have done

But if you put your mind to it
There still might be some hope
And with the help of others
You can get off the slippery slope.

I think this is a lyrical poem
I think that's what my teacher said
I think that's what my partner wrote
I'm almost certain that's what I read.

Bryn May (13)
Ripon Grammar School, Ripon

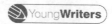

Untitled

The time waster,
The all haster,
The fall lopper,
The rebellion stopper,
The Magellion teacher,
The school's preacher,
The ghoul's ghost,
The not most,
The woman's nightmare,
The man's suicide,
The lad's reality,
The girl's reality too,
The cot wisher,
The pain disher,
The grain picker,
The happiness licker,
The wackiness enducer,
The drug end-user,
The bug poison,
Feed on my soul,
They beat on your soul,
And give nothing at all,
But when I reach my goal
They'll take one final fall,
Homework.

Calum Richardson (11)
Ripon Grammar School, Ripon

The Chase

You can hear the heavy breathing
But you are still reaching
Running, running
Your feet are drumming
Eager to be away
But weariness weighs you down
You're struggling, straining
Desperate to escape
Your feet are flying
The land a blur
Over stream
Over hill
Through valley and vale
The chase continues
Your breath is heavy
Your feet are slowing
You urge yourself on
Faster, faster
The panting behind you
Louder and louder
Nearer and nearer
But you are away
There are wings on your feet
You're surging ahead
To safety!

Ciarán Steele (12)
Ripon Grammar School, Ripon

Colours

Black is the dark night,
Wolves hunt in the deep black night,
Black is in the air.

Blue's the morning sky,
Blue is the colour of waves,
Blue's the deep blue sea.

Green's the colour of grass,
Cows munch on the cold grass,
Green leaves fall from trees.

Red are tomatoes,
Red is the colour of blood,
Red's like sweet strawberries.

White is like sticky glue,
White like a polar bear,
White is like thick snow.

Yellow stars at night,
Yellow fireworks exploding bright,
Yellow colours write.

Colours burst in fright,
Colours of a bright rainbow,
Colours die at night.

Jack Burton (11)
Ripon Grammar School, Ripon

The Golgy - A Mythical Creature

'Twas inkled in blithey blotches,
Creamished with slavering whiffles,
Sheened and blasteringly angled,
The Golgy whimpers and riffles.

Its craggy whistle collabed in,
'Bally, bogroh, bafil, beware!'
'Wamil, wafoo, warble, wickful!'
The Golgy boomed in despair.

Donna Castle-Ward (11)
Ripon Grammar School, Ripon

North Yorkshire & The North

It's Not Fair

It's not fair.
Me and my friends go somewhere.
We are told to go away.
So we do.
It's not fair.

It's not fair.
Me and my friends go somewhere.
We start a game of cricket
Then Scary Mary comes out.
Guess what?
We are told to go away.
It's not fair.

It's not fair.
Me and my friends go somewhere.
We start a game of football.
We are not being told to go away!
It's going too well.
Oh no, someone's coming.
We are told to go away.
There is nowhere else to go.
It's not fair.

Luke Robinson (13)
Ripon Grammar School, Ripon

Just Because . . .

Just because I don't smoke dope, doesn't mean I'm not cool.
Just because I won't go clubbing, doesn't mean I'm a girly girl.
Just because I like James Bond, doesn't make me violent.
Just because I'm not religious, doesn't make me bad.
Just because I try at school, doesn't make me lame.
Just because I'm quite clever, doesn't make me a nerd.
Just because I'm small, doesn't mean I'm silly and stupid.
Just because I support Man Utd, doesn't make me a glory supporter.
Just because I don't like chocolate orange, doesn't make me fussy.

Just because I am who I am, and shall ever be.

Henry Way (11)
Ripon Grammar School, Ripon

Got Soul?

Ba bum the beat of the heart
Voosh impaled with a dart
Should kids be playing with a gun?
Ask their leaders who whip, torture . . . kill.

These kids, they need some fun
Just killing . . . to kill it's the scum of the Earth
Put the murder to mute
Not ever taught to execute
Why people think it's a thrill
It's the scum of the Earth to kill.

Men, women and *children*
Their minds will burn,
Their guts churning in the blender of . . .
Love, yes, surely one day.
Love, protection for the young.
Think of the world . . . love.

So rare is this word, so rare.
Flying around like a single dove
This is the word, *love* . . . shout it out
Hugs to the world, happiness . . . peace.

Dashiell Barnes (13)
Ripon Grammar School, Ripon

One Day

One day I found the shop that sells the best hot chocolate.
One day I saw a bursting pot of gold at the end of a rainbow.
One day I felt kindness and love.
    One day . . .
One day I smelt hope in the early morning.
One day I believed what I couldn't see.
One day I felt I could climb the highest mountain.
    One day . . .
One day I met the person that doesn't care what you look like,
Where you live or how different you are to them.
    One day . . .

Lydia Bakes (11)
Ripon Grammar School, Ripon

English Class

I sit here in class, bored out of my mind,
I sit here trying to think of a rhyme,
Like a punishment for an unknown crime,
I sit here clueless, not knowing what to do,
Escaping every minute to go to the loo,
I sit here stiffly in my plastic chair,
Playing with my tangled hair because I don't really care,
I sit here in a room full of pupils talking,
As the teacher drones on about nothing important,
My head drifts off to a land far away,
A land we reach in our dreams,
I wonder what it's like to be in the clouds,
Where I'm never asked to read aloud.
'What's the answer?' Miss knows I never listen.
'. . . Oh, I don't know,' is my favourite reply.
'Oh dear, that's a shame.'
Why do I always get the blame?
Maybe it's the teacher, who knows?
I sit here in class staring out of double glazed glass,
Who knows, maybe one day I'll get a pass.

Hannah Scholes (12)
Ripon Grammar School, Ripon

Pure Evil

He lurks in the dark just waiting to pounce.
On that poor little mouse, he has taken an ounce.

His eyes are slit, he blends in the dark.
Those dogs should have waited 'til he was out of the park.

He crawls round the corner, raring to go,
And get the dinner he doesn't deserve, you know!

The mouse! That innocent animal,
Creeping into the hole, but is now not at all.

Loving and caring because of that *cat!*
He is now inside the small, smelly flat.

Emily Peirson (11)
Ripon Grammar School, Ripon

Black And White Keys

Separated from the world by a single sheet of music.
The notes are written, the ending planned out, no, I disagree.
My fingers find their place, my heart alongside them.
A way of expressing myself only my mind understands.
I begin to play a smooth melody.
Taken over by the sensation my mind loses itself in the music.
Sudden thunderclaps erupt from the pages.
Shattering all worries.
I continue to play my symphony of black and white keys.
I quickly change from a fierce tiger to a sleek cat.
Memories flood back to me from within my soul.
I am suddenly sat, alone, with no company but the whistle of the wind.
And then by chance, my senses emerge.
I am back at the uneven keys.
My temper rises; I play the notes hard enough to break down a door.
And then, I stop.
Tears fill my eyes.
Too many dreadful memories lie in wait at this ebony piano.
And then, I leave, abandoning the black and white keys
Full of heartless thoughts of despair.

Julia Atherley (11)
Ripon Grammar School, Ripon

My Love

Love is the fruit on the trees, the wind in my face
and the clouds billowing past; as vague as my childhood.

You are the flowers blossoming to me, the very smell,
the very scent of a rose;
sparkling its true majesticism out towards the world beyond.

Mother Nature bows down to your beauty
as you walk past, as graceful as an antelope.

Your pure radiance shines out from everyone else's.
Among the mass of bright stars, you are the brightest.
You are: my love . . .

Sean Bartlem (11)
Ripon Grammar School, Ripon

Red Is . . .

Red is . . .
Red is the beautiful sunset
Red is a fisherman pulling in his last net
Red is a pack of fresh steaks
Red is watching while dawn breaks
Red is a brilliant, amazing view
Red is your lost family watching over you
Red is the awesome colour of glory
Red is listening to a wonderful story
Red is the sound of huge church bells
Red is travelling merchants attempting to sell
Red is a delicious apple crumble
Red is Captain Coconut's jingle mumble
Red is the blood that drips from a mother deer
Red is its children watching in fear
Red is the sunset concluding the day
What a wonderful place to stop . . . and pray
Red is my favourite colour out of them all
Because in the end, it's so big, mighty and ever so tall
Red is . . .
Joe Brown (12)
Ripon Grammar School, Ripon

Grey

Shades of grey
Dull
Boring
No excitement
No movement
But . . .
A ray of sunshine
A shimmer
A stirring
Be happy
Just a little.
Imogen Fowler (15)
Ripon Grammar School, Ripon

Spreading Smiles Round The Sun

Around the world, some places I've seen,
Teeming with tourists all glad to be free,
From their everyday work, in an office maybe,
Or as a full-time mum drinking her seventh cup of tea.

Yet often we forget,
The people who collect,
Into a very large number,
They suffer from hunger,
And thirst, no slumber,
No shelter, nor money, nor healthcare.

They've no chance for holiday,
No chance to go out and play,
No chance to be bored in a lesson, perhaps,
They don't get to learn, they just work for some scraps.

It doesn't seem fair,
It doesn't seem right,
But it *can* be overcome, if we all do our bit,
So let's all help to try and spread smiles round the sun.

Sophie Veitch (12)
Ripon Grammar School, Ripon

Stupid Similes

The little boat floated . . .
As well as a bowling ball wouldn't.
The snow, freshly fallen
Was as white as snow.
As the car shot by so quick
The police pulled it over for speeding.
Frank and Gemima had never met.
They were like two hummingbirds that had never met.
The cold, still fossil of that dodo
Was as dead as something lacking life.
This is the end of the poem
Not the start . . . obviously.
Once upon a time . . .

Alex Gath-Walker (16)
Ripon Grammar School, Ripon

Black Clouds

My purple glasses caused quite a stir,
Because apparently I looked like a nerd,
So I said back to them, 'So, I don't care,'
But that really wasn't the right thing to say.

The next day at school they followed me around,
They picked on me and then I found myself on the ground,
Now why was I there? It was them of course,
They took off my glasses and threw them in a bush.

So when I got home my mother went mad,
She said, 'Oh why are children these days so bad?'
But I said to her, 'Did it happen to you?
Do you really know what I have been through?'

She then said to me, 'Oh yes, I do know.'
So then she told me her tale of woe,
And after that I felt a lot better
Because black clouds always blow over.

Maria Isabel Scullion (11)
Ripon Grammar School, Ripon

Death

It spreads.
It spreads its giant hand,
To freeze the warmest hearts in the cold and barren land.
It breathes.
It breathes with icy breath,
With all the dead souls that have fallen towards it.
It takes.
It takes anyone,
At any time, to its cold and distant past.
It moves.
It moves from place to place,
Taking all who are destined in a short space of time.
But it recoils.
It recoils from a spark,
The single spark of brightness that is hope.

Jessica Rutherford (12)
Ripon Grammar School, Ripon

Bubbles

Bubbles.
Slowly growing, inside my chest
Worst day of my life - or maybe the best?

Falling.
Opponents around me - I want to win
Feigning my confidence, but trapped within.

Bursting.
Can't see a thing, the room is a blur
The judges are gone, they want to confer.

Blowing.
There is a voice, I can just hear
The world seems to stop, my vision is clear.

Bubbles.
Inside my body, my worry uncurled
I can do anything, my oyster - the world.

Naomi Fowler (17)
Ripon Grammar School, Ripon

Butterfly

I am the queen of small,
I flitter, flutter by.
I pause,
I rest
And dance till morning nigh.
I flit, from flower to flower,
I flitter, flutter by.

I am the queen with wings,
I flitter, flutter by.
I show my happiness.
In graceful swoops,
And light the morning sky.
I turn the skies sweet not sour.
I am the butterfly.

Thomas Bowe (11)
Ripon Grammar School, Ripon

The World Just Carries On

The wind does blow
and the sun doth glow.

When the heav'ns do flash
the hail does crash,
the world just carries on.

When the weather's harsh and
they hide away like Simon Cowell.
They don't act so free,
so don't end up listening to you or me,
so the world just carries on.

When the night comes along,
and no one does belong.

The mum and children snooze,
and the dads sneak out to grab some booze.
But still the world just carries on.

Derek Van Der Westhuizen (13)
Ripon Grammar School, Ripon

Nightmares

Lying in bed, parents out all night.
People screaming, shouting,
Messing around outside my window,
Shadows in the garden.
Hear things downstairs, creaking of doors,
Clattering of pans.
People in the attic playing with the toys,
Throwing the boxes,
Breaking precious items,
Mum's vases, Dad's garden gnomes,
Brothers' plastic snowmen.
My door creeps open,
Someone's shadow at the door . . .
It's Mum and Dad!

Harry Cleary (11)
Ripon Grammar School, Ripon

Distant Desires

Far away in a distant land,
A child filled with fear is forced to fight.
His proudest possession is his menacing gun,
He has nobody to guide him on what's wrong and what's right.
They've taken his family, they've taken his freedom,
What more has he got to give?
A ruthless life without laughter and love,
I wonder if he knows how the other half live.

Snug and safe in my wealthy world,
My life is filled with promise and pleasure.
Shopping, sport, computers, clubs and television,
All these things and much more I can choose at my leisure.
I can feel free and go out with my friends or stay in and play,
But I always ask for more.
Feeling peace in my secure surroundings,
I must never forget the woeful child at war.

Annabelle Blyton (12)
Ripon Grammar School, Ripon

War Is No Game

David stares at the screen as he plays a game.
His fingers rapping at the buttons on the control pad.
Bang! Bang! Another enemy dies.
David wins the game, and it's a new high score.

Abu stares into the darkness, his life is no game.
His fingers grasp the trigger of a gun.
Bang! Bang! His tortured mind is filled with terror.
Abu is a child soldier and this is war.

One boy's play is another boy's reality.
No escape for Abu. The bad men make him do it.
Both life and death are fearful to him.
David doesn't know the truth.
He has never known pain like Abu.
If he had, would he question,
Should war ever be a game?

Alexander Speight (13)
Ripon Grammar School, Ripon

If Only I Could . . .

If only I could blend into the shadows,
What then?

If only I could slowly fade from this world,
What then?

If only I could get away from this deep dungeon,
What then?

If only I could find a way to make my dreams into reality,
What then? Happiness?

If only I could . . .
. . . Then maybe, just maybe,
I could find where I belong!
I could find where I am loved!

But right now, I can only dream,
But then, just what if . . . ?

Georgina Brewer (14)
Ripon Grammar School, Ripon

Green Is . . .

Green is the greatest view,
Green is the heart inside you,
Green is the limey zing,
Green is the rapper's bling,
Green is the mightiest mountain,
Green is the chocolate fountain,
Green is the tallest tree,
Green is the buzzing bee,
Green is the shining sun,
Green is the cream bun,
Green is the big blue sky,
Green is the luscious steak pie,
Green is the Great Barrier Reef,
Green is the world with no grief,
Green is the parrot's wing,
Green is the greatest thing.

Jack Baker (11)
Ripon Grammar School, Ripon

Trapped

I am sitting all alone,
I am only skin and bone,
I am frightened, but I have hope.
I watch the children laughing, playing and having fun,
While getting hot and sticky from the summer sun,
I wish I was out there, just like them,
So they are lucky to be free.
I know that I have hurt my mum and dad,
But does that really mean I'm bad?
I am sorry, I am sorry,
Please forgive me, please,
They need to see me.
I am sorry for what I did.
I am sorry that I hid.
My family are so dear,
But why did I choose to be trapped in here?

Holly Oldham (11)
Ripon Grammar School, Ripon

Forgotten Deeds

I'm in trouble again,
But what for this time?
I'm waiting, wondering.
What could be my crime?
Was it about the window?
If it was, there must be a rat.
Maybe it was about me smoking?
No, they couldn't know about that.
At last I was summoned,
Into the dragon's lair,
I was as quiet as a mouse
And I trod with care.
He stood there,
Towering above me,
Then he realised his mistake,
It wasn't me in trouble, it was Lee!

James Woolfenden (14)
Ripon Grammar School, Ripon

- North Yorkshire & The North

When I'm With You

When I'm with you I am soaring
I am hiding the joy inside
But I cannot hold on to it any longer
A diffusion of light and happiness
Is going on in my heart
I am the piano always playing a melody
Swirling, twirling, dancing
Jumping, twisting, dropping
Collapsing in a heap on the floor
Exhausted from laughing with you
Rising, rising, swooping, laughing again
I feel like the drum that never stops
I am the highest note a bird can sing
I am the chord that echoes and echoes in every note
In every happy song.
That's what you make me feel.

Leah Carling (12)
Ripon Grammar School, Ripon

Fireworks

I sit . . .
    Watching . . .
        Waiting . . .

Suddenly a
    Bang,
        A pop,
            And a big burst of colour.

Blue, red, yellow,
    Glowing in every direction,
The sparks dance in the starlit night.

Finally the show ends . . .
    The happiness in children's faces linger
As does the glow from the dying embers on . . .

Bonfire Night.

Emma Armstrong (11)
Ripon Grammar School, Ripon

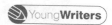

Random Comments

'My grandad was in the second world war.'
'So was mine.'
'Mine was only a child.'
'My dad's been promoted.'
'My sister's doing her GCSEs.'
'We've got a new car.'
'My computer's broken.'
'Where's my homework gone?'
'I hate maths.'

Silence.

'Why's everyone making random comments?'
'Hypocrite!'
And the babble recommences.

Peter Walker (12)
Ripon Grammar School, Ripon

What I'm Going To Write About

I'm not going to write about sandals,
I'm not going to write about beards,
I'm not going to write about tropical fish,
I'm not going to write about blood.

I'm not going to write about stick men,
I'm not going to write about chocolate and sweets,
I'm not going to write about books.

I'm not going to write about penguins,
I'm not going to write about sport,
I'm not going to write about washing your feet,
I'm not going to write about gloves,
Which strangely leaves me with nothing more to say.
Sorry about that.

Matthew James Pimley (11)
Ripon Grammar School, Ripon

Breast Cancer

(This poem is dedicated to my mum.)

Oh no! Oh no! The dreaded day
You go to the doctor and he says, 'OK . . .'

Unfortunately, it is bad news,
But it is easy to repair, it's only a fuse.

Go to the hospital every three weeks,
They'll put a syringe in your hand,
And you'll probably shriek.

It's in there, for three hours straight,
You'll just have to sit there, 'Oh great!'

After six times of sitting there
You'll go back home, with no hair.

George Robinson (12)
Ripon Grammar School, Ripon

Human Nature?

Man is top of nature's food chain,
No real predators, so nothing to fear;
Yet not content we fight each other;
Millions are killed every year.

What is at the root of all this warfare?
Why do we fund endless weapon advance?
Ever more deadly, secretive, expensive;
Politicians argue, peace groups dance.

Is it all because we are scared of difference;
Politics, lifestyle, our gods or skin?
Why do we cling to those just like us,
Instead of understanding all as kin?

Oliver Colville (12)
Ripon Grammar School, Ripon

Love

Love pounces on you like a tiger,
It makes your heart go ping.
It makes you feel excited
And makes you want to sing.

Love bounces inside you like a ball,
It makes you scared and mad.
It makes you feel so weird
And makes you stressed and sad.

Love flounces and dances like a falling snowflake,
It makes you happy and content.
It makes you amazed and jumpy,
Love is a good friend.

Emily Brook (11)
Ripon Grammar School, Ripon

Without You

Without you . . .
    flowers would never bloom,
    the brightest light would be overshadowed
    and my heart would never beat again.

Without you . . .
    spring would never come,
    school terms would never end
    and all music would disappear.

Without you . . .
    birthdays would never come
    the sun would never shine
    and I would die a slow, painful *death*.

Bethany Abel (11)
Ripon Grammar School, Ripon

Black Is . . .

Black is a rainy day.
Black is nothingness.
Black is emptiness.
Black is . . .

Black is midnight.
Black is magic.
Black is darkness.
Black is . . .

Black is the freezing sea.
Black is evilness.
Black is the colour I love!
Black is . . .

Elliot Fearn (11)
Ripon Grammar School, Ripon

I'm Not The Person

I'm not the person to walk from a fight
but I'm not the person to start one.
I'm not the person to say I'm smart
and I'm not the person to say I'm dumb!
I'm not the person to say I'm in love
even if I was.
I'm not the person to take drugs
even if my friends does!

Why, just why does everyone bother me?
I don't think it's fair.
I wish there was a place for me.
I know there is, somewhere.

Alexander Vanzo (11)
Ripon Grammar School, Ripon

Scars Last Forever

Bang!
The sound of the gun
Rattling through the air
Then it's silent
Quietly the birds sing
Not aware of what's happened
One man: no longer
One wife: now a widow
Two kids: now fatherless
A scar through their hearts
And scars last forever.

Thomas Stringer (12)
Ripon Grammar School, Ripon

Untitled

I'm waking up,
I'm feeling red,
Red is . . .
Red is a murderous sky,
Red is a dragon's fire,
Red is a tall spiral overhanging a street,
Red is a wolf's high stance,
Red is the dullness of the world,
Red is . . .
I'm feeling red,
I'm falling back to sleep.

Samuel Atkinson (11)
Ripon Grammar School, Ripon

Sorry

Sorry, didn't mean it,
Sorry, I won't do it again,
Sorry, it was insane,
Sorry, it can't be that much pain.

Sorry doesn't clear it, although I use it now and again,
Sorry sometimes causes that pain,
Sorry is a foul word, pointless if you ask me,
Some people hate saying it over again,
Well here's a tip,
Try not giving them that unbearable pain.

Ryan Wood (11)
Ripon Grammar School, Ripon

Family

Members of family are very important to you.
Sisters are sometimes annoying, sometimes useful.
They are sometimes a waste of space but sometimes fun.
Brothers are sometimes stupid but sometimes clever.
They are sometimes playful, sometimes life-savers.
Mums are sometimes grumpy, sometimes nice.
They are sometimes warming, sometimes cold.
Dads are sometimes sporty, sometimes lazy.
They are sometimes selfish, sometimes they spoil you.
Members of your family are very important to you.

Max Oliver Vesty (11)
Ripon Grammar School, Ripon

Many Children

Many children without a childhood,
As they have been stamped in the mud.
Many children wanting to be loved,
But they've been used to being shoved and shoved.
Many children covered in cuts,
Some friends say, 'If you want freedom, get some guts.'
Many children are abused with anger and hatred all tied in knots,
But they want people to think about them and help them lots and lots.
Let's help those innocent children out there
And put them back in loving care.

Thomas Whitaker (12)
Ripon Grammar School, Ripon

A Day At The Races

I backed a horse at
ten to one, it came in at
a quarter to four.

The bookie told me
that I was a fool, he said
I should bet again.

I said that he steals,
he said he was genius.
So I backed another.

Will Forbes (16)
Ripon Grammar School, Ripon

Pollution

Car fumes fill the area and attack the ozone layer.
Ink-ridden waves kill the crying seagulls, hundreds every day.
The bright blue sky turns duller and greyer.
The sun gets hotter and burns like fire.
The trees overwork to produce more oxygen.
Penguin homes melt away into the ocean.
Streets fill with litter and smother the Earth.
Clouds disappearing ever so slightly.

Stop polluting now!

Bethanie Archer (11)
Ripon Grammar School, Ripon

Snaps

It's amazing how easily family snaps
Become like pictures taken by the paps

Flicking through those glossy pages
How little you can relate to the frosty faces

Remember those celebs'll never last
Unlike what happened in your past

Bright lights can blind what you're feeling
But your family should always be more appealing.

Emily Horner (15)
Ripon Grammar School, Ripon

Midnight

M ysterious ghosts roam the gloomy streets.
 I n-between the shadows stray cats lurk.
D ustbins crash as they seek for food.
N ameless souls float in the night sky.
 I n churchyards zombies moan and groan.
G reen and maggot-filled as they emerge from their graves.
H igh above in the bare trees ravens roost.
T onight is Hallowe'en.

Tom Beaumont (11)
Ripon Grammar School, Ripon

Fireworks

F ire bolts firing into the sky,
I rresponsible teenagers setting rockets and bombs off,
R ockets running into the dark, gloomy sky,
E mptying gunpowder as they burn away,
W andering, winding sparkles getting thrown around,
O range, blue, red sparks jumping about,
R unning, jumping children as they go bang,
K nock, bang, crash! go the fireworks,
S taring at the wonderful colours.

Miles Butterell (11)
Ripon Grammar School, Ripon

The New Girl

There's a new girl in my class,
I hate her so much,
There's a new girl in my class,
She acts like she has no sense of touch,
She sits in my chair,
She's got really wacky hair,
There's a new girl in my class,
She's driving me . . .
Mad!

Molly Aikman (11)
Ripon Grammar School, Ripon

It's Not Fair

It's not fair that we are forced to go to school
It's not fair that adults make the rules
It's not fair that adults say you don't know what to do
It's not fair that adults think we don't know who is who
It's not fair that we get told off for everything we do
That includes going to the loo

Adults, we don't care what you think of us
Because there is more to us than meets the eye.

Daniel Williams (11)
Ripon Grammar School, Ripon

Help Me

Help! I feel I'm alone once more,
Help! I'm going backwards, not forward like before,
Help! I feel like I'm in a world of my own,
With no way out, not one at all,
Help! My head's spinning round and round,
As I ask myself why I feel so homebound.

I need some help, some assistance please,
To help me through this crisis I currently see.

Katie Treasure (11)
Ripon Grammar School, Ripon

Trapped

I'm trapped, nobody knows what I feel like inside.
I'm trapped, stuck in a rat trap and no one to let me out.
I'm trapped, not going forwards or backwards, just still.
I'm trapped, nothing coming or going through my head.
I'm trapped, stuck like a tree but not growing or shrinking.
I'm trapped, dry like concrete, letting people walk over me.
I'm trapped, nothing here or there, just a black room.
I'm trapped, please help!

Jacob Turner (11)
Ripon Grammar School, Ripon

Nightmare

Having a nightmare is horrible and scary.
Just when a warty witch comes out called Mary.
Or when the wild lion comes in
Or when the red Devil reveals himself
And lets out his sin.
But then you wake up
And you feel relieved.
But then you realise that it's just starting.

James Andrews (11)
Ripon Grammar School, Ripon

Walking In The Night

The cool spring nights
The stretched clouds
Float slow
Making the moon's face
But not its glow.

Here I am
Walking slow
Strangers' heads down
Ignoring the crowds
I hear a sound
The cat miaows
Alone
Awake
Abandoned . . .

I see a crowd
It's quiet but
Feels loud
I'm just stood there
Alone
Awake
Abandoned . . .

Home is in sight
Welcoming under the street light
I'm no longer
Alone
Or
Abandoned

And no longer awake
Together
Tuckered out
The family
Together.

Elizabeth Jones (12)
Salford City Academy, Eccles

The Hamster Dragon

My hamster was having babies
We were going to have some more
Until the egg came out of her
I had never seen one of these before.

It was golden, smooth and shiny
An unusual egg for a hamster?
But until it cracked,
We couldn't see what was packed
Inside the strange egg.

Two days after . . . an arm,
Slightly popped out of the shell
I still wasn't sure if it was actually a hamster
No, I couldn't really tell.
Inside the strange egg.

Its arms and legs pushed out
Another two days after that
Whatever it was, girl or boy
I decided to call it Pat.

Finally the creature arrived
I couldn't believe what I was seeing.
A dragon came out of my hamster
Which is like an ant having a human being.

All I could see was teeth
As sharp as a hedgehog's back
Was it a friendly dragon
Or was it going to attack?

No it was a friendly dragon
I could tell by its crystal-blue eyes
As blue as Titanic's necklace
Except they change colour when *she* flies.

Courtney Newton (12)
Salford City Academy, Eccles

Untitled

Waiting all day in line
Hoping tickets will be mine
Five hours went by
A stranger came and said hi
'Is the line small?'
'I don't know, I'm not tall!'
It's four in the morning
It's so boring.
Eating McDonald's breakfast this early,
We met a woman named Shirley.
Sleeping in sleeping bags
People smoking fags.

It's getting light
It doesn't feel like night
Looking around
With people is all I see
There isn't room for you and me
But look, I'm here
Some dude watching 'Top Gear'

Front row seats
That you can't beat
Stood right at the stage

I got my tickets
I feel so great
I really can't wait
Till December 28th

Natasha Tomlinson (14)
Salford City Academy, Eccles

My Poem

Autumn wind upon my face
As the leaves rush past me furious to race

Suddenly the street lights light up
When I'm walking down I take a sip from my hot chocolate cup

I rush home as it starts to get late
Then my phone alerts, it's a message from Kate

The lights from a car take over my eyes
I hear a dog barking, whimper and cry

I'm finally home, it took a while
But as I walked in I saw a warm smile

It was Kate, she had thrown me a birthday party
She walked over to me very smartly

A kiss on the cheek and a birthday hug
I was showered with presents, one of them was a mug

This is a night I will never forget
And that long walk home . . . I'd never regret

Finally everyone goes home
But I have to tidy up so I kind of moan

How could I moan? It was such a great night
But I think, *those car lights have done something to my sight*

I tuck up in bed nice and snug
And have a sip of tea from my new mug.

Faye Lengden (12)
Salford City Academy, Eccles

The Desert

Here I am walking through the desert.
Sand, sand is everywhere.
Hot, hot, the sun is beaming down on me.
Drip-drop, the sweat is running off my face.
As I walk further and further along the sand,
That's when I hold my head in my hand.

Nicholas Cluley (13)
Salford City Academy, Eccles

I Hate Sundays

Get up, watch telly
2 hours later bored silly.
Long day, don't know
What to do.
God I hate Sundays
They're poo!
Play on my Wii to kill
Some time.
My sister wants a game
I say, 'No, it's mine.'

Now 2.30, time for lunch
I'm now so fed up I need
Something to punch.
Lunch over, wash up
Back in front of telly
Wish I hadn't eaten so much
I've got a sore belly,

Shower, get things ready for Monday.
Off to bed to get some sleep
Goodbye Sunday.
Hooray!

Alexandra Cowlishaw (13)
Salford City Academy, Eccles

The Derby

Man U and Man City's derby is here
Everything has paid off, every sweat and every tear,
With the likes of Rooney, Evra, Giggs and Scholes
We've left City hanging with the 4th and final goal
In the Premier League table Man U are very top
City won't stop trying and will be playing non-stop
When Berbatov shot, Given got the ball
He threw it to a player who was not very tall
When United won, everyone was happy
Except for City's manager, he was an unhappy chappy.

Josh Farrell & James Looker (15)
Salford City Academy, Eccles

Why Don't You Care?

I tell you what I am thinking,
That he is not good enough for you.

He robs and takes drugs,
He smashed up your car, he's just a thug.

I am so down, I have cut my wrists,
I wish I could punch him with my fists.

How can you love him
After everything he has done?

He has ruined my life,
Isn't that enough?

Why do you only care how you feel?
Why don't you care about me too?

I want him out of our lives,
He doesn't deserve anyone.

I just want you to tell him you want him gone,
Please just think about me for once.

You don't deserve this much hurt,
If you tell him to go we can be happy, please.

Bethany Downie (13)
Salford City Academy, Eccles

At Sea - Haikus

As I walk upstairs,
To see the metallic door,
I grab the handle.

As I walk forward,
The harshness of the cold wind
Stops me in my tracks.

As I look for land,
There is nothing but the sea,
I feel so alone.

Saul Whittle (14)
Salford City Academy, Eccles

Deep Down In The Jungle

Bang, rumble
Deep down in the jungle,
Plants and leaves,
Insects and trees.
Who knows what lies in the jungle?

Rats, mice,
Things not nice,
Tigers roaring,
Before the day is dawning.
Who knows what lies in the jungle?

Lions, giraffes,
All things daft,
The dawn is breaking,
The insects are shaking,
Who knows what lies in the jungle?

Snakes, tyrannous and strong,
Never wrong,
The fire's burning,
The wind is whirling.
Who knows what lies in the jungle?

Katie-Jayne Leggott (12)
Salford City Academy, Eccles

The Third World

The Third World is like a dream to me,
But think about the people that would have been too scared to flee.
Their houses aren't made of bricks and mortar,
They have to travel really far just for some water.
They have to walk far
But we use a car.
Think of the families whose children are dying.
How much would your mum and dad be crying?
They don't have a phone to text for help,
I bet if your life changed to theirs
You wouldn't know what to do next!

Natalie Harwood (12)
Salford City Academy, Eccles

Three's A Crowd

My dad walked out on me at the age of four
I remember the police knocking on my door
'Police! Police!' they'd shout and ball
'There's nobody here by the name of Paul!'
I'd sit there in my room and cry
Days, months, even years went by
Then a new man came on the scene
His name you ask, well it was only my uncle Tim
My mum claimed that he wasn't my real uncle
And that they had met years ago down at the gym
But that's when it started
He'd get angry and well he'd hit my mum and me
I asked my mum could we move out
But she said no we will sort things out,
But she didn't
So I took it upon myself
A teacher at my school told me to ring Childline, so I did
A lady named Julie helped me out
She told me how to cope with things
And three years later we're as happy as can be
My mum, my rabbit and me!

Natasha Roebuck (12)
Salford City Academy, Eccles

Rainbow

It is this rainbow season
That love fills friends' hearts
Some to express, some to hide
Some to broadcast, some are shy
You shouldn't hide and you shouldn't be shy
Nobody's gonna laugh at your lovely lines
Oh, beautiful rainbow, beautiful sign
Forever having her by my side.

Kaylie Devine Williams (13)
Salford City Academy, Eccles

Truth Of Lie

Is the value of truth worth more than the security of the rosy stories fed to us every day? What is its value? Is the whole truth even possible, or wanted? Many of us live in a world where the truth is perverted into something that is more opinion than truth.
We live in a masked world that takes joy in rosy outlooks.
Reality is way too painful. Love is truth.

You thought . . .

I had the responsibility,
that I had the ability,
to care and love, just tell the truth,
but simple I was as a youth.
Then the expected truth began to prove,
our love just faded and moved.

We couldn't see through the star,
changing the colour of the sky.
is it over or out?
I've still got doubt,
part of me is dead,
this love's killing me.

Malek Abdo (12)
Salford City Academy, Eccles

If I Were Rich!

What would I do if I were rich?
I would spend, spend, spend
But not a penny on you!
I would buy for my mum, dad and maybe my little sis too.
A gate for my house, so grand and tall,
67 bedrooms in all.
Imagine the sleepovers with all of my friends
We'd keep the butler busy, that's for sure.
Spencer, the butler, could sleep in the shed
To rest his head.
Well my dream is a dream which maybe is extreme
But one day you'll see it's all true.

Amy Richards (13)
Salford City Academy, Eccles

Dead And Gone

There I was, stood there still, waiting for it,
Then it came, the hardest punch of the year,
From the girls who had bullied me all my life.
I fell to the floor, kicks and knees were hurled at me.
Hitting my head and body.
I opened my mouth to scream,
But nothing came out, there was just silence,
They stopped,
I got up and ran.
I thought they had finished.
I turned and looked back,
They threw a big rock,
It hit me *hard* in the head,
I fell to the floor,
Smacking my head, hard.
I lay there, still.
Battered and bruised.
Not moving at all.
Then formed a crowd of people trying to help me,
They couldn't, I was gone . . .

Leoni Sufyaan (13)
Salford City Academy, Eccles

Drugs, Guns and Needles

Drugs, guns and needles are crime,
On the street with Stanley knives.

The police, ambulances and fire brigade
Are doing their job whilst afraid.

They are looking behind after each step they take.
But they can't help not to shake.

A fight in the chippy and a fire bomb in a car.
999 is busy all the time.

Teenagers with hoods up and knives down their backs,
They work with druggies with cocaine and smack.

Louis Edmonds (12)
Salford City Academy, Eccles

They Choose Me

They choose me cos of my friends,
And because I do my best,
They choose me cos of my levels,
Forget about the rest
They choose me cos of my glasses,
And because I want to do well,
They choose me cos of my religion,
It hurts me what they tell
They choose me cos of my feelings,
And because I'm never late,
They choose me cos of my lifestyle,
But their lives are full of hate
They choose me cos of my clothes
And because I have many fears,
They choose me cos of my opinions,
But they laugh, they cry tears.
They choose me cos I'm different,
So I know I'll never win.
But just because I don't say anything,
Doesn't mean I've given in.

Melissa Louise Robinson (13)
Salford City Academy, Eccles

My Poem

Saturday is here
It's always the same
Come 3 o'clock
It's time for the game
Cheering on your team
Your voice is hoarse
That's if your team is winning of course!

Jody Entwistle (13)
Salford City Academy, Eccles

Bully

Like a thorn in my side
I've nowhere to hide
You've got a sting in your tail
And you'll get me without fail.

Is it my hair, my size, my shoes?
Whatever, I'll always lose
Tell you what's wrong, I'm sure we can sort it out
But you'll rather get angry and shout.

There's a name for you, you're a bully!
If I'm not to your liking you'll tell me with your strife
It's not just verbal but the physical abuse too.

I pray to God that this will end
But now I'm older and wiser
I saw you the other day walking down the street
No more do I have this pain in my side
It's now your turn to run away and hide
No longer do I have this thorn in my side.

Katie Halliwell (12)
Salford City Academy, Eccles

But That's How I Am . . .

The sky is blue,
But that's just how it is.
The grass is green,
But that's just how it is.
Clouds are fluffy,
But that's just how it is.
Life can be tough,
But that's just how it is.
Sometimes feelings get hurt,
But that's just how it is.
Sometimes hearts get broken,
But that's just how it is.
I'm different to you,
But that's just me.

Ellie Scott (14)
Salford City Academy, Eccles

Untitled

It's the match of the year,
And everyone's in fear because it is one-all
A free kick here and a free kick there,
Just because of a hand ball,
The referee blows his whistle
Just outside the area,
The keeper shouts so very loud,
Well I ain't scared of you.
He strikes the ball with force and power
But the keeper stops it like a tower
We're now in penny shootout,
This shot could win the match
I really hope the keeper
Doesn't dive and make a catch
I hit that ball with my strength
It feels like ages from the length
Finally the ball's in the net
This amazing height I won't forget.

Jack Redford (12)
Salford City Academy, Eccles

Grandad

You may be ill, you may be weak
But one thing I know is you ain't no geek
You will fight the battle and you will win
You always have and you always will
I'm sure in our hearts there's a space
That you can call your special place
You have so much to live for
Life's not a game, and if it is, you played yours well
But now you're near the end
Our support is strong, your strength is weak
But together we will reach the highest peak
So give your kisses and say your goodnights
Unfortunately you're going to sleep forever
So let's turn out the lights.

Emma Tombling (13)
Salford City Academy, Eccles

Four Seasons

Winter, the snowy time of year,
Cold and frosty,
The children cheer.

Spring, bright and colourful,
Flowers start rising,
They all look wonderful.

Summer, time to have a laugh,
Picnics on the beach,
Breakfast in the café.

Autumn leaves start to fall,
Orange, red and brown,
Trees are bare and tall.

Rochelle Johnson (13)
Salford City Academy, Eccles

Untitled

Oh England, oh England
You are my country
Oh England, oh England
Surrounded by sea

Oh England, oh England
The weather's not great
Oh England, Oh England
At least we have mates

Oh England, oh England
We're very funny
Oh England, oh England
And we've got money.

Jack Nicholson (12)
Salford City Academy, Eccles

Skateboarding

I like skateboarding
And I can do something
A Nollie, a manual and a flip
And I nearly broke a hip
So beware
Do not fret
But don't skate wet.

I skate mongo
I don't do regular
I go to skate around Green Street
And in the game Skate I take no defeat.
Because my skating is pretty neat.

Daniel Edwards (12)
Salford City Academy, Eccles

Dear Bully

Dear Bully,
Why do you hate me?
I haven't done anything wrong
Please could you just stop.
It's been going on for so long.
Why did you . . .
Record me getting hurt,
And then show the whole school?
You thought it would be just a laugh
But you made me into the fool
Why did you . . .
Steal my friends away from me
And turn them into you?
Just could you stop it, stop it, stop it now.
Can we look past this and start a new?
How would you feel?

Bryony Chapman (12)
The Read School, Selby

What Do I Think Of Me?

If I'm not super skinny or really fat
If I wear jeans instead of trackies,
What will they think of me?
If I don't shout out rude words,
If I like school,
What will they think of me?
If I don't have any drugs or alcohol,
If I don't paint and scribble on walls,
What will they think of me?
If I don't steal those cigarettes,
If I don't get in that fight,
What will they think of me?
I've seen what happens to people like me,
Their lives are made a misery,
So let's just wait and see,
What do I think of me?

Phoebe Simpson (13)
The Read School, Selby

Hope

Cancer is a killing curse,
It brings out only the worst,
Cancer's the world fighting against you,
All you want is to say, 'Shoo!'

Cancer is like a monster eating away at your body,
Take the treatment and you will be fine,
If it's your family support them and help them when needed,
Care for them and help them through it.

Cancer makes you feel,
Like you have been given a raw deal,
Family and friends are so kind,
I will beat it in my mind.

Everything will be fine!

Katie Poskitt (11)
The Read School, Selby

Popularity And Bullying

If I were a popular person I would play with my friends,
Kick a ball with them,
Share jokes and laughter.
If I were a popular person
I would have an ally by my side
He would stick to me like a magnet
Whilst sharing pain and joy.
If I were a popular person I would be over the moon.

Horrible hair,
Freckled face,
Short in stature,
That's what they say,
But bullies never benefit.

Luke Rayner (11)
The Read School, Selby

Kids' Crime

Kids smoking is like the Black Death,
Kids smoke, kids die,
You'll never see your loved ones again,
Keep your children under your rules.

Kids carrying knives is the world's end,
It will destroy their lives forever,
It is a crime you can't forgive,
So stop it now or they'll be sorry.

Instead of children destroying their lives,
Teach them the right way of life,
They don't know better,
Unless you show them how.

Victoria Leigh (11)
The Read School, Selby

I Just Want To Be Me

I do not want to be labelled,
I am not a thing,
No one can tell me who I am.

I do not care what you say,
I am not perfect,
But I am not imperfect.

I do not think you're clever,
Treating me like this,
Stop! I just want to be me.

Megan Victoria Hughes (12)
The Read School, Selby

But Why?

But why do teenagers get bad publicity?
But why do 10-year-olds murder people?
But why do gangs carry guns?
But why do gangs carry knives?
But why do their knives kill people?
But why do they carry on killing?
But why do the people of the world smoke?
But why, *but why?*

Chris Porter (13)
The Read School, Selby

Cancer

Cancer can kill
Cancer is like a monster trashing people's lives
Cancer affects loads of people's lives
Cancer is an evil curse haunting people's lives
Cancer could affect you
Cancer can kill
Cancer cannot always be cured.

Jenny Stauffer (11)
The Read School, Selby

Assault

A ssault hurts
S wiping at you
S upreme pain
A ssault hurts when it's
U nprompted
L ightning-fast punch
T aunting to hit back.

Alex Tant-Brown (11)
The Read School, Selby

My Sports

Gymnastics on a Monday
Over the vault I go
Netball on a Tuesday
In the net the ball goes
On Wednesdays I go trampolining
Up and down I spring
On a Thursday I do volleyball
Around the court I go.
On a Friday I have a rest
All ready for Saturday.
On Saturday again it's gymnastics
A floor routine I do
On Sunday I need all my rest
Before I start the week again
As I'm constantly on the go.

Emma Farrington (12)
Walkden High School, Worsley

The Elements

Fire
Fire is the warmth we hold
The passion, the anger and the fear.
Fire is the fiery Hell
Or the heart to do something.

Water
Water is the shimmering sea,
It is the perfect twin for fire,
For its clouds all anger
Water soothes and holds you for all eternity.

Earth
Earth is the provider of nature
It brings death and destruction
It will also bring life
Earth will bless us and hold us.

Air
Air is the darkness that holds us,
The light that brings us life,
It is beautiful and gleeful,
For he is all to see.

Death
Death is the dark woman,
Who clouds all light,
Her spirit will remain forever
Although her heart is locked away.

Edward Hughes (12)
Walkden High School, Worsley

Uncle Phil, My Codfather

When I was smaller than I am today
There was a game we used to play
It was the swing you used to do
This time in 10 years I'll do you

As I got bigger we had to change
This year we took you to a range
At Heatherton - oh no, a gun
But in the end it turned out fun

Archery, pistols, clay pigeons afar
And with that gun you was a star
In the contest we all were hist'ry
We put it down to all that whisky

On the canal you took me fishin'
To catch a pike, ha, we're wishin'
But on your own, a photo to mark it
I think it's in a supermarket

You are decisive - at least we think so
Come on Phil, it's time to go
To leave the house takes you an hour
Where is he now?
He's in the shower!

We go for walks pretty far
As long as we have our breakfast bar
Over hill and down dale
In the sun or usually hail

Oh and the dogs, they must come too
Just so that Meg can do a do
They run further, a little tidge
Like Rosie did at Wiseman's Bridge

You see, we all went out for the day
But left with Phil, she ran away
He told us later that all was fine
But only after a little wine

Distarhyme - North Yorkshire & The North

On holidays with car and tackle
To fit in clothes it is a battle
A rod for this, a rod for that
Shell and the kids? I'll pack a hat!

I love Uncle Phil, he is a star
He lets Auntie Shelley drive his car
Foot off the brake, forward they creep
Then in reverse, what's that beep-beep?

My uncle Phil works very hard
So I think it's only fair
That sometimes when we visit
I find him sleeping in his chair

I think I'm usually very good
But I must declare
That sometimes my behaviour
Makes you shout and swear

We both have our good points and also a few bad
I would like to say thank you, for all the fun we've had
I am lucky to have an uncle, so special and so rare
I appreciate all you do and know how much you care.

Thank you.

Adam Peacock (12)
Walkden High School, Worsley

A Messed Up Poem

My life is dull and boring,
But some days very bright,
I've not got school tomorrow,
So my day will be light,
I've got to tidy my room today,
So I can play on my broom,
Oh no my brother broke it,
He nearly broke my door too,
And he can roar,
As loud as a dinosaur,
And he nearly broke the law today,
He smacked my mum,
He smacked my dad,
So guess what,
He got a big, fat *whack!*

Amy Broome, Jenna Millership & Amy Masters (12)
Walkden High School, Worsley

I Want To Be A Lawyer

I want to be a lawyer, there's nothing you can do
I also hear that they don't eat stew
They get a lot of money
Which isn't very funny
And if they win the super case
They don't get sprayed with mace
And if they don't
Then people won't
Laugh and hate
Their once old mate
That didn't win the super case
And didn't get sprayed with mace
Will still get the money
Which isn't very funny.

Jack Corrigan (13)
Walkden High School, Worsley

Say No To Drugs

I sit here gorging out of my head
I took some skunk and went to bed
I need some drugs to make me better

I have no money
I have no friends

I had loads of money
I had loads of friends
I wasn't on drugs then

Don't take drugs cos it's killing me
It has killed my friends
It has killed my family

Say no to drugs if anyone offers you some.

Jake Allison (13)
Westlands School, Thornaby

Mum

I love you
Whenever I saw you
You would put a smile on my face
You made me laugh
When I was feeling down
You cheered me on
When I was doing good
You made me laugh
You never gave up and you kept trying
You never let anything stand in your way
That's why I love you so.

James Coates (13)
Westlands School, Thornaby

Heal

Cuts will heal, words will not
They build inside like a blood clot
It's addictive like a whisky shot
He follows like a sheep
But none can see the pain deep inside
Problems with his mother and father
He feels he is in deep lava
It burns inside like heartburn
All he says is it's none of your concern.

Joshua Waller (13)
Westlands School, Thornaby

Emotions

I have no emotions
Nothing makes me sad
Apart from deaths when this is my mum and dad
Sometimes I'm happy
Sometimes I'm sad when something happens to my mum or dad
Sometimes I'm angry
Sometimes I'm aggressive

But I'm still me: Accept me for who I am, not what I do.

Billy Hill (13)
Westlands School, Thornaby

Grandad

Some days when I am down
My mum always makes me smile
Except from this one day
When my grandad was poorly
I cried because I thought he was going to die
I hate being right.

Matthew Taylor (14)
Westlands School, Thornaby

My Summer Holiday!

My summer holiday!

Every year I go to Spain,
For my summer holiday,
I go with my family,
And in the sea we love to play!

My summer holiday!

I stay in 'Apartamento Prealsa',
It has its own beautiful pool,
And the sun is always beaming down on us,
So the water keeps us nice and cool!

My summer holiday!

Our resort is Benalmadena,
But we like to go to Mijas,
And I even bumped into Georgina,
Who is in my tutor class!

My summer holiday!

We love to go to a faraway beach,
So for the past few years we've rented a car,
We love the huge, crashing waves there,
And there's wonderful restaurants and bars!

My summer holiday!

We always love to go and see the dolphins ,
They put on an amazing show,
They flip and twist and balance on their tails,
How they do it - nobody knows!

My summer holiday!

As three weeks in Spain is nearly over,
And our holiday is coming to an end,
I'm thinking of all the fun we've had,
As I don't have any euros left to spend!

My summer holiday!

Katy Jenkins (11)
Whickham School, Whickham

At Last

Autumn, autumn time is here,
The time for change,
The time for fear.

The fresh morning dew, asleep on the grass,
The short, dim days,
And heavy rain falls en masse.

Acorns and sycamore seeds lie neglected on the ground
Inside cosy little shells,
Oblivious to all and any sound.

An earthy-musty smell suffocates the air,
Engulfing the sweet summer fragrance,
Which made the hot days easy to bear,

The birds sing their gentle lullaby,
Perched safely on a tree,
Surrounded by sky.

Now I can feel fear,
For my time has come,
And the end is near.

The wind is in torrent,
A ferocious dragon,
Building up to its moment.

Then it happens, I break away,
In less than an instant,
To the ground I sway.

There I lie,
Crisp but damp,
The question is; who am I?

Autumn, autumn time has passed,
Change has happened,
The fear has gone . . . *at last*.

Francesca Louise Best (12)
Whickham School, Whickham

My Awkward Life

I was nervous today - my first day of school.
I told myself, everything will be OK.
It will be OK.
Will it?

In the playground I fell over; started to yell.
Today in art I punched Katie McBell.
Well it was her own fault really, she stole my glue,
Because someone painted her nose bright blue!

I didn't want to come to school today,
Because my pet cat called Nala had run away.
She was always sneezing, as if she had a cold,
So at school today I was as good as gold.

I was anxious today, the Christmas play!
I told myself, it will all go well.
It will go well.
Will it?

Mary and Joseph both wanted to put Jesus to bed.
They tugged and tugged and off came his head!
The head knocked Wise Man 3 unconscious,
(I think it was Katie McBell's brother).

I've got my SATs results today,
According to my results I failed 2 exams on Friday.
I couldn't concentrate, the weekend ahead!
Above all that, I needed my bed.

I was feeling scared today - my first day of college
I told myself, everything will be fine.
It will be fine.
Will it?

My life is very awkward, things keep going wrong,
Especially now that I've just got expelled.

Jennifer Thomson (12)
Whickham School, Whickham

We Are Friends

We are friends, like sun and moon,
Just like one big flower bloom.
The sea, the sun, the waves, the sand
Together we hold hands.
Round the circle once and twice
Then once again thrice.

We are friends, like sky and grass
Like one colourful wine glass
We meet each other every day
And listen to what we have to say.
We talk about funny things
But no one knows what the future brings.

We are friends like black and white,
We stick together day and night
All the things that we have done
We have had so much fun.
We dance, swim and trampoline
In everything we are very keen.

We have been friends for a long time
If we aren't together we sometimes pine.
I hope we will always be together
And our friendship will last forever.
We have gone through so much
But all the time have been in touch.

Flowers may die and suns may set,
But year after year I will never forget.
I will always remember a friend like you
Me, myself and I even you too.
We have been together since we were young,
And have climbed the ladder rung by rung.

Kaitlin Sophie Fiddler (11)
Whickham School, Whickham

Normal?

What is normal?
Being all the same
Living in a grey world
Where no one is ashamed?
Should I just fit in
Or shout my statement proud?
Should I dress like you
'Cause it's cool
Or is it okay
To go my own way?
Why do you bother
Acting cool?
'Cause all you're doing is
Being a total fool.
Should I follow the trend
Or start my own?
Should I do what you do
'Cause that's what's now?
Can I say no
Or will you mock me?
Do you really give a damn
About who I am?
In this world today
Should I go or should I stay?
I am what I want to be
You can't change me
I'm not asleep
I don't follow the herd
I make my own.

Jack Stewart
Whickham School, Whickham

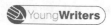

Should It Be This Way?

As I walk through the grounds of the school,
Getting pushed by those I call fools.

I dread to wake up on a morning,
As I wonder what's next to come;

Pain!
Torture!
Aggression!

Should it be this way?

As I walk through the grounds of the school,
Getting pushed by those I call fools;

I hate to walk to lesson through the day,
As I would probably get thumped on the way;

Pain!
Torture!
Aggression!

Should it be this way?

As I walk through the grounds of the school,
Getting pushed by those I call fools;

As I detest to get my dinner on a lunch,
Without a doubt; there will be a punch;

Pain!
Torture!
Aggression!

Should it be this way?

Hannah Shield (14)
Whickham School, Whickham

Imagination Land

He found himself in the middle of a town
With just his wallet and his dressing gown
He thought to himself, *where on Earth could I be?*
All but buildings he could see.

He walked out of the house, still very much dazed
His mood would not change, it was a very long phase
Then what should he see but his old classmates
Gathering outside the school front gates.

He stumbled past the deteriorating school
Thinking he was a bit of a fool.
Soon the school was out of sight
Still staggering, like he had just been in a fight.

He picked up a paper and looked at the date
The year was 1998.
He simply could not believe his eyes
He was sure that he was in a world of lies.

Surely nothing could be less true?
At the thought of this, his face turned blue.
He saw some youths, who looked rather flimsy
They were smoking like a chimney.
They reminded him of his forgotten rage
For he had started smoking at a very young age
He tried to warn them of the damage that could be done
But when he told them they thought it was fun
He suddenly woke up inside a hospital bed
With not a memory in his very blank head.

Conor Gillespie (13)
Whickham School, Whickham

I Want Never Gets

I'm going to buy my first set of wheels,
Off to the garage I go to check their deals.
I want a car that's sleek and fast,
But when I get there the choice is vast.

I'm pleased my driver's test I've passed,
But know I mustn't drive too fast.
I still want a car to steal the show,
And not an old one that goes too slow.

I'm going to buy my first set of wheels,
Off to the garage I go to check their deals.
I want a car that's sleek and fast,
But when I get there the choice is vast.

Maybe a convertible like an Audi,
So I can put the roof up when it's cloudy.
I want one with horsepower you can't ignore,
And when you count the turbos they equal four.

I'm going to buy my first set of wheels,
Off to the garage I go to check their deals,
I want a car that's sleek and fast,
But when I get there the choice is vast.

Then I see it - the car of my dreams,
It's black, it's slick - it's perfect it seems,
The salesman says it's perfect for me as the driver,
I count my money - bother - I'm short by a fiver.

Daniel James Smith (12)
Whickham School, Whickham

Family

F eelings of love and loneliness,
A nger and disappointment,
M emories of the past,
I am proud to be part of them,
L ove them for who they are,
Y ours I will always be.

Rebecca Horsfall (11)
Whickham School, Whickham

Acrostic

A nguish, like a tree crackling in a spine-chilling storm.
B raveness, as a quandary comes to mind,
C owardice, like a gladiator shadowing away from his opposition.
D elicate, a flower, seconds away from snapping.
E nemies, cutting into you like sharp daggers.
F rightened, like a field mouse trapped in a bush fire.
G enuine, nothing left to lose.
H eartbroken, as someone smashes your heart.
I mpulsive, wanting to get back up.
J ubilant, you're building yourself up.
K indness, gives you the reassurance you need.
L oved, it's a nice feeling.
M entioned, letting you bounce up to the moon and back.
N osey, are the people snooping around you
O verjoyed, like winning a gold medal.
P ositive thinking, that's how people get places in life.
Q uite content, it's nothing unpleasant.
R ain, pouring down on your smiling face.
S elf-conciousness, it isn't an issue here.
T rees, ripening with apples and oranges.
U nderstood, as people see through the coating.
V ery engrossed, at how people can change their minds so suddenly.
W onderful, a balloon lifting you to the stars.
e X cellent feeling when you're ecstatic.
Y elling in excitement, like on a roller coaster.
Z ealous, fanatical feelings.

Niamh Reading (12)
Whickham School, Whickham

Anonymous

By anonymous . . . who could that be?
A silent stranger the world can never see.
Do they write a poem, speech or a book?
What's the point, no one even looks
Are you ashamed of who you are?
Don't hide because we know you're a shining star.

Samantha Wynn (14)
Whickham School, Whickham

Just One?

'Just one sniff'
'Just one drink'
'Just one kiss'

Look into the future
Where your life will head,
If you listen to these people who
Ignore what their parents have said.

You're a raging alcoholic
Who spends all day in bed,
You don't smell perfume
But you smell drugs instead.

You have a dead-end job
With very little pay,
And you spend it on wine
At the end of the day.

Some people call you a loner
'Cause you have no friends,
Not at home or at work
And that's how it ends!

'Just one sniff'
'Just one drink'
'Just one kiss'

It's your future, you decide.

Kate Farrey (12)
Whickham School, Whickham

Sport

S wimming is my game
P laying football is my dream
O ptimistic is what I want to be
R unning is my hobby
T ennis makes me really happy.

Kaylea Steadman (12)
Whickham School, Whickham

Autumn Days

A tickling, misty miracle
Comes out tonight,
And now the little apple tree
Is captured in frozen light.

Upon the icy branches,
A frosty film is caught,
With trailing threads of leaves,
Polished patterns wrought.

The autumn clouds wander,
Peering through the light,
This silver horizon,
Across the frosty blue night.

A dazzling icy window,
And crystals are the spider's web,
Exposed in the autumn bed.

The grass is tassels,
The trees jewel-sown,
The sycamore seeds spiralling down,
The morning dew taking the crown.

Such sparkle in the chilly air
Oh, can it be the darkness
That spoils it all and makes it oh so bare?

Caitlin Leigh Jefferson (12)
Whickham School, Whickham

Him

He may do his homework but he's not a nerd,
He doesn't do drugs or follow the herd,
He has lots of friends and does lots of sports,
So why won't the others just give him a thought?
He is often left out by the 'cool' of the 'crew',
He is who he is, they should be too,
There is no point in them acting cool,
But when it comes to class they are the fool.

Oliver Leathard (12)
Whickham School, Whickham

Change

Crisp, red leaves fall to the ground,
With just a gentle fluttering sound.
Gentle winds brush the leaves, not wild.
Like a mother comforting a child.
Rabbits prepare for hibernation.
Rats are huddled in the bus station.
People raking up leaves in the yard.
With the winds blowing it seems pretty hard.
Birds migrating for the winter.
As the cold weather begins to splinter.
Stray dogs shiver on the side of the street,
Waiting, hoping for a winter treat.
Now the snow begins to fall,
Nothing can be seen at all,
The air is just so icy cold
That it affects all, young and old.
Changes happen now and then,
And soon it will be spring again.
With all the baby lambs so bright,
It really is a lovely sight.
Winter, summer, spring and fall,
Will these changes stop at all?
No, they won't for death and for birth,
Because it's the beauty of our planet, Earth.

Lucy Wallwork (13)
Whickham School, Whickham

Football Till I Die!

F ootball is one of my favourite sports.
O h when I scored a magical goal from the halfway line
O h when I went to my first England match they won three nil.
T wo years in a row I've scored 18 goals for Whickham Fellside.
B ut when I went to my first Newcastle match they won two - one!
A t the start when I started playing football I scored 22 goals.
L osing is not an option
L oud, cheering fans trying to get on the pitch.

James McColl (11)
Whickham School, Whickham

North Yorkshire & The North

How To Be Imperfect!

I know, I know you've told me a million times
But I can't help it.

I sometimes stupidly lose things,
I usually look untidy,
I'm almost always in a wacky mood,
I can't awlays spel things corretcly,
I have some annoying habits,
I show off in front of important people,
I'm usually mean to my little sisters,
I can be outrageously loud,
I can moan enough to drive people crazy,
I'm hopeless at adding things together,
I have messy writing (even though I try),
I absent-mindedly use the wrong toothpaste,
I like some pretty lively styles,
I sometimes get scared,
I'm a bit lazy with my homework.

We can't all be perfect.
I guess I'll stick to being my stupid, untidy,
Wacky, annoying, show off, mean, loud, crazy,
Hopeless, messy, absent-minded, lively, scary,
Lazy self
Being imperfect is good enough for me!

Emma Foster (13)
Whickham School, Whickham

My Horse

My horse is as gentle as a lamb
She likes to eat hay and apples
She likes to go jumping
She especially likes the mud.

She is called Carrie
She is as naughty as my sister
I am very happy to ride her
And I'm as happy as a bee!

Niall Sutherland (11)
Whickham School, Whickham

Under Pressure

Peer pressure and blackmail, It's all over these days
To make teenagers go in these awful ways
Stealing, killing and taking drugs,
Seems like everyone's catching the bugs.
The evil is everywhere, you cannot hide
A house? A home? A hole outside.
But if I say no would they laugh
Or still really be my friend?
Would they think I'm uncool, a coward
For not following the trend?
It's pushing down on us constantly
Day after day.
And I mean it when I say
'Someone will pay!'
For there will be a day
When these deeds are undone
And the weights on my shoulders
Will soon be gone.
But till then I will wait
And hold my head high.
I won't let this stop me
From reaching the sky.

Sophie Drury (13)
Whickham School, Whickham

Bullying Worries

Don't let your worries get you down
Don't let the world get you in a frown
Cos it doesn't even matter what people say
You know you'll get through it anyway.
The words they may hurt, but just ignore and keep strong
Because you know you'll never be in the wrong.
Always be yourself, because you know who you are.
Following a crowd doesn't get you very far.
Life is a game, and it's meant to be played.
So don't let your problems lead you astray!

Jordan Oloman (14)
Whickham School, Whickham

On The Night Of Hallowe'en

On the night of Hallowe'en,
I was walking through the street.
Everything was quiet,
Not a word, not a sound,
Not the greedy little children running from house to house,
Not the easy-going parent tagging along behind.

On the night of Hallowe'en,
I was walking to a house,
Knowing the house was empty,
90 per cent sure.
I reached for the door handle taking a deep breath
My foot stepped onto the manky carpet,
There was no turning back.

On the night of Hallowe'en
As I looked around the house,
I saw nothing,
Everything was too black.
I heard a sound snapping,
I didn't know where it was,
I stood there helpless,
There was nothing I could do.

Mollie Pugmire (11)
Whickham School, Whickham

Sprint Race

S print as fast as a cheetah
P repare for the whistle
R ush for the finish line
I am so confident
N ow it's time
T he race is going to begin.

R un to the win
A chieve the win
C hallenge the others
E ncouragement from the crowd.

Callum Jones (11)
Whickham School, Whickham

Look What You've Done!

As they walk down the path,
Six in their group,
Cans in their wrath,
And scuffing their boots.

They pass through the park,
Shouting up to the heaven,
Ill manners they bark,
Now six has become seven.

They stop at the shop wall,
And paint it with sin,
Rude comments they call,
As they finish the gin.

But stop! Wait here,
The old folk sigh,
Watching them near,
In their old coat and tie.

Your generation started this clan,
And now you've finished your run,
You were where it all began,
Now look what you've done!

Ross Norman (13)
Whickham School, Whickham

I Remember

I remember I used to fight and get broken noses.
I remember I bullied people and made their lives miserable.
I remember I smoked, because I thought it would make me look cool.
I remember I never thought before I acted and got myself in big trouble.
I remember I used to be an alcoholic, I couldn't stop drinking.
I remember I scared people and threw stones at their windows.
I remember I had bad grades, and it forced me to live on the streets.
I remember I got expelled from school for doing what bad kids do.

But now I have changed, I am as nice as anyone can be,
It just goes to show that even the worst of people can change, like me.

Elliot Anderson (12)
Whickham School, Whickham

Being A Teenager

So being a teenager can be quite hard,
For simple reasons your life just changes,
Your friends, school and people,
They all then see you from different ranges.

So then you go school,
Trying not to break a rule,
You're just playing it cool,
Until the big bully comes along.

It's not like I have no friends, I do,
They're really sweet and kind to you,
But I don't stick up myself in front of the bully
Would you?

But then evening's fine when I go out tonight,
I'm with all my friends, everything's alright,
But then that bully comes, she starts a fight,
I walk away, I'm alright!

So there you have it,
It's not that easy,
It can drive you into a lot of havoc,
All of that bullying can make you feel really queasy.

Abbey Humphreys & Emily Higgins (13)
Whickham School, Whickham

My Dreams And Friendship

Friends since year 2,
Protected when I had no clue
I dreamt of friendship.
And that friendship dream came true
I am still her friend, but will it end
When we fall out, we're like cats and dogs
Then we're friends, because we said sorry
I love my life, it's more than I want
I've been created to live a very excited life
I couldn't ask for more than I have, I love my life and family.

Sarah Blacklock (12)
Whickham School, Whickham

Unknown Emotions

The world is full of people,
But you can still feel alone,
With feelings of love, pain and hatred,
It can be hard to cope on your own.

Adults try and listen,
But hardly ever understand,
And when there's no one there for you,
Things can get out of hand.

Adults think a teenager's life is easy,
But that's not always true,
It can be filled with emotions,
That at times can be troublesome too.

Talk to a friend you trust,
Don't let your feelings hide,
Adults can't always help you,
And don't always take your side.

Friends can help you through times,
When people don't care,
They can lift the weight off your shoulders,
And make life easier to bear.

Emma Crabtree (12)
Whickham School, Whickham

Footballs

F ootball is class
O ut on the field
O thers running around you
T ackling so much
B all on the ground, kicking it around
A ll playing the game
L ooking at the ball
L ooping it is
S coring a goal.

James Thompson (11)
Whickham School, Whickham

The Dangers Of The Night

The dangers of the night,
Haunt everyone in sight,
Scary masks and costumes too,
No one discovers who is who.

The dangers of the night,
Give little children frights,
Don't worry little child,
Do not listen to the wild.

The dangers of the night,
Moths flapping in the light,
Bats screeching in the dark,
Cats prowling in the park.

The dangers of the night,
Vampires come out to bite,
Do not worry, do not fear,
Stay with those who hold you dear.

The dangers of the night,
Are gone in broad daylight,
Live your life, have lots of fun,
Looking after number one.

Alice Arbon (11)
Whickham School, Whickham

What is Bullying?

What is bullying?
Bullying is hard to go through,
Being alone, no one likes you because it's 'uncool'.
What is bullying?
Bullying is lonely, thinking you're the only one,
What is bullying?
Bullying is something you don't want to happen to you,
What is bullying?
Bullying is horrible!

Sophie Mansel (13)
Whickham School, Whickham

Life Is Better Without Addiction

I was once a teenager,
That was long ago,
After being days without drugs,
I was at an all time low.

I had just smoked a joint,
A very foolish crime,
I was off my face when they found me,
And I was sentenced to do 6 months of time.

My life wasn't so good just then,
Sitting in a rotten jail,
All my friends were using their money to meet their addictions,
So they could afford to pay my bail.

After I had done my time, I was sent to rehab,
They made sure I didn't go back to my terrible ways,
It took a while to get used to
But getting unhooked took days.

I'm glad I quit,
I've lived a long life,
There was one person who helped me more than anyone,
My caring, loving wife.

Alex Luke Franklin (13)
Whickham School, Whickham

Astronomy

A lways succeeding as my favourite subject,
S tars and constellate look like objects
T remble as the gravity attracts you
R ambunctious activity makes you aroused
O rion's arm grasps you with might
N eptune's angle will make you perplexed
O nly light is the way to travel
M eteors bombard you with unimaginable force
Y oung stars ready to be born.

Tadiwa Forster (11)
Whickham School, Whickham

Friends

We were best friends,
But not anymore
Having a fight
Isn't a good thing at all,
Alone in the yard
With no one beside my side
If only I had a friend
Beside my side.

On the way home
I walked alone
But a small, shy, boy walked behind me,
I asked for his name,
He said it was Daniel.
Now I know his name
I sat next to him in class

And walked back home with him every day,
I had him over for dinner,
And for tea.
He's always beside my side like two brothers,
Until he became a teen.

Jordan Hudson (13)
Whickham School, Whickham

Thirteen

I am quiet, doesn't mean I'm a loner
I get good grades, doesn't mean I'm a swot
I don't do drugs, doesn't mean I'm a loser
I don't smoke, doesn't mean I'm not cool
I don't cause trouble, doesn't mean I'm not a laugh
I do dance, doesn't mean I'm queer
I don't fight, doesn't mean I'm feeble
I like to play football on the street, doesn't mean I'm intimidating
I come home looking dirty, doesn't mean I've had a fight.

I am thirteen and I am who I am and don't care what other people think of me.

Marcus Bell (13)
Whickham School, Whickham

Street

Graffiti is all about publishin' ya soul,
So let your soul speak and spray it on the wall,
It's usually advertised on the train lines,
So let the art flow out their youthful minds.

Knife crime is one of the biggest crimes today,
So get it off the streets and start to obey,
On the streets of London, it's beginning to rise,
The blades of knives are doublin' in size.

Drugs and drink are becoming a teenage action,
So let's reduce the chance to the smallest possible fraction.
It damages your liver, it destroys your brain,
So what's the point in doin' it?
It only causes pain.

The kids are scared to go out on the street,
Because that's the place where the gangs meet,
They come in their hoodies with their knives hanging out,
All they can do is swear and shout.

Take this rap into consideration,
And just team up to take over the nation.

Keir Redfern (14)
Whickham School, Whickham

Teenagers

We all have one picture in our minds about teenagers:
All teenagers take drugs,
All teenagers hang around street corners,
All teenagers intimidate others,
All teenagers commit horrible crimes,
All teenagers have ASBOs,
All teenagers steal things,
All teenagers smoke.
That's what old people think we are like, but
All teenagers aren't like this
It's just a couple of thugs that set the scene for all of us.

James Dobson (13)
Whickham School, Whickham

Litter Is Everywhere!

Litter is on the ground,
Litter is always found.
Litter is in the car park,
Litter is in the dark.
Litter is part of the rules,
Litter is dropped by fools.

There's litter in the trees,
It's killing lots of bees.
Seagulls wheel round,
And squeal in the school grounds,
Flies hover over the bins,
Which are filled with tins.

I don't know why people do it,
My mum says people who litter should admit it.
I get angry when I see litter,
It should all be put in one big cellar.
There's litter everywhere in the school,
People do it because they think it's cool.

Litter is everywhere!

Nathan Haley (13)
Whickham School, Whickham

Untitled

My mates never leave me
They're always there if need be
We always have a ball and none of us are very tall!

Me and my mates are like a chain that can't break
We all like to drink milkshake!
We love to bike all night
And we think it's right.

We love sweets
And we know all the cheats
We're never late
So come on, give us a rate.

Nathan Johnson (11)
Whickham School, Whickham

The Roller Coaster

The excitement,
The fear,
The butterflies in your tummy,
You're just about to go, when you scream,
'Mummy, Mummy, Mummy!'
Your head's thrown back at 100 miles per hour,
The adrenalin is pumping, you start screaming louder and louder.
You go up the hill, then down again, then upside down
Into the corkscrew,
In the tunnel, out the tunnel,
Round and round we go.
Who knows when it's going to stop!
Looking ahead there's a sudden drop,
We scream, we laugh, we nearly cry,
It makes you feel as if you can fly,
As we get thrown from side to side.
We can see it's nearly the end of the ride,
We do our final loop the loop.
As the brakes screech we know the ride is done,
I'm definitely coming back on here, that was so much fun!

Sarah Beggs (12)
Whickham School, Whickham

My Friends

My friends are the best, they beat the rest.
We play games, sometimes we get amazed.
Our favourite drink is Diet Coke, you know it's the best drink.

My friends make a ring, they make your ears ding,
They are so loud they make you proud, ring-a-ding-ding.

My friends play for a footy team, they all play for a different team
They are all good players when they try their best.

The live not too far from me but it's like they live around the world.

That's the end about my friends, do not forget they are the best
You pay your respect, my friends are happy like a jar of honey.

Elliott Shattock (12)
Whickham School, Whickham

Maybe

Maybe I listen to different music.
Maybe I wear different clothes.
Maybe I have an unusual style.
Maybe I am not popular.
Maybe I am not as sophisticated as you.
Maybe I am quiet, like a mouse.
Maybe I think before I act.
Maybe I am not as rich as you.
Maybe I don't have 'the looks',
Maybe people don't like me.

'There she is,
The kiss-up!'
'Goth girl's coming!
Hide!'
'Don't look at her!'

This happens to her every day,
But everyone is equal.
Treat each other with
Respect.

Rachel Taylor (13)
Whickham School, Whickham

What If?

What if the world was at peace?
What if there was no war?
What is there was no crime?
What if there was no killing?
What if there was no hatred?
What if there was no peer pressure?
What if there was no depression?
What if there was no aggression?
What if there was no respect?

Teenagers, we're not bad people,
We respect what we have,
We're not what you think we are.

Caitlin Bray (13)
Whickham School, Whickham

Tests!

Tests
They drive you up the wall
Tests
You sit in your chair,
Nobody talking
Tests
The silence is like a silent scream
Tests
You work hard,
All year you work hard for them
Tests
The timer is ticking
Tests
You think about your future,
What you think you'll be
Tests
Briinng!
The timer has gone
The grades finally come . . .

George Henderson (12)
Whickham School, Whickham

Autumn

Autumn; when the days are short and the nights are long,
When the trees are bare but the leaves are colourful,
When rain pours and morning dew glistens on the green grass,
And animals begin to hibernate.
The night of Hallowe'en, where greedy, red-faced children
run around the streets in costume,
The ghosts and ghouls come alive,
As the lantern gleams brightly
Bonfire night when fireworks fly high in the sky,
And crack, bang and fizzle into magnificent colours,
And mounds and heaps burn down to the ground as ashes.
But as December soon comes along,
The end of autumn comes along.

Luke Rogers (11)
Whickham School, Whickham

Teenagers

The old woman scowled as I strolled down the road,
What a horrible hag she is, you'd think I was a toad!

People think we might do drugs,
When really they're the great big mugs!

Sometimes we are not to blame,
When you find we're all the same.

When you see us in our youth,
Then you'll see we're telling the truth.

If you remember your younger days,
And how your mates used to behave.

We want to have fun with our friends,
We like to laugh and follow trends.

We love to spend time with our families,
To celebrate birthdays and make memories.

So next time you see me on the road,
Try and smile at that ugly toad!

Francesca Riani (13)
Whickham School, Whickham

Not A Fighter

I sit back and watch the world go by,
I don't really want to try.
I see people destroying their lives
And people telling unforgivable lies,
Taking drugs,
And becoming thugs.
Is this what the world is coming to?
You see people fighting,
Going behind bins and lighting
So this is why I don't try
And sit back and watch the world go by
And the reason why I do this.
Is that I'm simply not a fighter.

Emma Martin (13)
Whickham School, Whickham

Even If

Even if some young people carry knives,
And go around claiming people's lives.
Even if some young people hang around in gangs,
Swearing, cursing, knocking over bins - *Bang!*
Even if some young people take drugs,
Doesn't mean we're all thugs.

Even if some young people like to get high,
And tell quite a lot of lies.
Even if some young people stay out till dark,
And start to light up around the park.
Even if some young people get in trouble,
Doesn't mean elders need a protection bubble.

Even if some young people cause chaos at the gates,
Doesn't mean we've all got awful mates.
Even if some people think they are cool,
By doing drugs and skipping school.
Even if some young people don't listen to what you say,
We aren't all that way.

Bethany Lowes (12)
Whickham School, Whickham

On The Night Of Hallowe'en!

Hallowe'en; out all night
Parents don't worry we're snuggled up tight
Trick or treat
Yum, gummy feet.
Loads of sweets
It just repeats.

In the night,
Don't give us a fright
Having fun, my bag weighs a tonne
As the night draws to an end
Monsters' costumes are in need of a mend
My sweets I'll not share
You'll have to wait till next year.

Jamila Ati (11)
Whickham School, Whickham

Why?

Why are there wars?
Why do people get killed?
Why are there guns?
Why? Why? Why?

Why is there bullying?
Why do people fight?
Why is there child abuse?
Why? Why? Why?

Why is there global warming?
Why do people kill animals just for their skin?
Why do families fall apart over something so small?
Why? Why? Why?

Why do people set fire to buildings and forests?

These are questions I ask myself every day
There is never an answer to them.
The most important question is . . .
Why do we let these things happen?

Amy Thoburn (13)
Whickham School, Whickham

Would He Love Me?

Would he love me if I dyed my hair?
Would he love me if I wasn't a swot?
Would he love me if I was on drugs?
Would he love me *if I wasn't me?*

Would he love me if I was cool?
Would he love me if I was older?
Would he love me if I smoked?
Would he love me *if I wasn't me?*

Would he love me if I was prettier?
Would he love me if I didn't get annoyed at simple things?
Would he love me if I had cooler friends?
Would he love me *if I wasn't me?*

Georgia Watkins (12)
Whickham School, Whickham

Two Minds Are Different

Bully
I am the one that gave you that black eye,
I am the one that made you cry.
I am the one that stole your money,
I am the one that made you look funny.
I am the one that picked on you,
And always thought, *what you going to do?*
I am the one that called you names,
But mostly I just called you lame.
I am the one that hurts you every day,
So don't you think I should pay?

Victim
I know you think that I am weak,
That everyone just calls me a freak.
Every day is like another war,
And I am sick and very sore.
So what are we going to do?
I will start, I forgive you!

Samantha Ion (12)
Whickham School, Whickham

Teenagers

All the news presenters
Say 'Hey, hey
All the teenagers are bad today,'
But we ain't all bad
Just the odd one,
But they're mostly wrong.

Mostly they're great,
Not to hate
We're honestly great
You should be our mate.

We don't do crime,
We just do time
For crime we did not commit.

Shaun Angus (12)
Whickham School, Whickham

Should I Be Afraid?

Should I be afraid to walk into school
Just because of one person
Somebody who is wrecking my life
And I can't let that happen

I tried to get on with things
But this monster won't let me
Can it not be helped
Or can I go free?

Should I be afraid to walk into school?
I certainly don't think I should
Should I stand up for myself?
I am wishing I would

I'm wondering whether I should tell someone
Or will that just get me in more bother?
I thought that I should, so I did
And the bully is now no hard kid.

Daniel Jackson (13)
Whickham School, Whickham

I Might

I have a fear of planes, doesn't mean I'm a wimp.
I might get high marks, doesn't mean I'm a swot.
I might get bullied at school, doesn't mean I can't stand up for myself.
I might have a unique style, doesn't mean I'm not normal.
I might wear glasses, doesn't mean I'm a geek.
I might wear no make-up, doesn't mean I'm ugly.
I might not play sport, doesn't mean I'm inactive.
I might wear braces, doesn't mean I'm a nerd.
I might be quiet, doesn't mean I don't have my own opinion.
I might be soft, doesn't mean I'm fragile.
I might not fight with people, doesn't mean I'm a failure.
Be who you are,
Don't let people tell you who you don't want to be,
Because at the end of the day,
Everyone has their own life.

Sophie McGovern (12)
Whickham School, Whickham

Welcome To Secondary School

Toilets, bogs, loos, lavatories
Let me tell you all my stories
Secondary school isn't worthwhile
Stupid jokes will make you smile.

Maths, science, English, history,
In the staff room there's a mystery
Pigeon holes full of detention slips
Only of kids' blabbering lips.

Dance studios full of mutter
If you go in there you're classed as a nutter
In and out of them girls go
Preparing for the variety show.

Bunsen burners, science labs
Hardcore radjis, smoking tabs
Of course there's always a gang of nerds
In the maths room learning.

Emma Iveson (13)
Whickham School, Whickham

Why?

I know I wear hoodies but I'm not a crook,
So adults shouldn't give me a nasty look,
I don't carry weapons like guns or a knife,
So why don't they let me get on with my life?
I don't go round fighting and doing drugs,
So why do we all get labelled as thugs?

If I wanted to drink, I'd go out and do it
But I know that I am too young at the minute,
I'm just a kid that's having fun,
Why do they assume that I've got a gun?
I'm not a druggie, I'm not a thief,
I don't need to turn over a new leaf.

Don't think I'm nasty because of how I look,
And don't just judge the cover of a book.

Lucy Watson (12)
Whickham School, Whickham

Green Is Gone

Evergreen and grass the only green,
Not a glint of sun can be seen,
Everyone dressing up for Hallowe'en,
The night when witches make you scream.

Leaves abandon trees - leaving them bare,
Sit in front of the fire in a comfy armchair,
The sun deserts me without a care,
The sound of crunching leaves is everywhere.

A splash of colour catches my eye,
Then the boom of fireworks up in the sky,
It doesn't matter how hard I try,
I can't turn away from the picture so high.

Autumn is a magical time,
The time when nature can really shine,
This season isn't just a pastime,
Because autumn is a magical time.

Charlotte Dunhill (11)
Whickham School, Whickham

Global Warming: I'm No Quitter

Aerosols and thick car fumes,
Landfill tips will bring our dooms.
In 50 to 100 years they say, I wish that thought would go away
Ice caps melting faster and faster,
I only wish that people would master
The fact we need to look after the Earth,
As we've been on it since our birth.

Rubbish and litter flying,
Soon we will be lying
In our trash from toe to head,
But instead . . .
We should help our world in many ways,
Be planting trees and picking up litter,
I wish it was that way, but all I know is, I'm no quitter.

Sophie Emily Turner (12)
Whickham School, Whickham

My Best Friend!

(Dedicated to my best friend Rebecca Ramsay.)

My best friend holds me tight,
My best friend kisses me goodnight.
My best friend loves me for being me,
My best friend won't let me be.
My best friend wears crazy clothes,
My best friend loves me loads.
My best friend knows when I'm sad,
My best friend isn't scared when I'm mad.
My best friend is sweet at heart,
My best friend is not smart.
My best friend gives me good advice,
My best friend is so sweet and nice.
My best friend is really strong,
My best friend is almost never wrong.
My best friend is in my heart to stay,
My best friend and I will never drift away.

Lauren
Whickham School, Whickham

The Competition

I got off the bus,
I was so nervous and frightened,
I waited with my friends,
I was shaking like a leaf,
I just wanted to get out there,
My first race was next!
All of my friends wished me luck,
I went to my race,
I was getting ready,
And the whistle went,
I was running and I got a stitch,
It hurt like a bullet going in you,
But I won!
I was proud as punch.

Charlotte Birkett (11)
Whickham School, Whickham

Young Days

When I walk through the streets,
Past all the drunken nuts,
I wonder how many people have damaged their guts.
Drinking and drugs are all very fine,
But if you do them, you are certainly not a friend of mine.
We all get blamed for things we're not.
Blame the older generations
For making things that make us rot.
The old hags and geezers are always giving us dirty looks,
But what if we were in a huge huddle, reading lots of books?
I'm sure they wouldn't mind that much anymore,
But what they have got to remember is,
That they were young a long time ago
Do they really want to make things go in slow mo?
We want to enjoy our young days, before it's too late,
So I hope you don't mind,
But I think I'll spend them with my mates!

Ethan Days (13)
Whickham School, Whickham

The Palomino Pony!

I have a horse called Fliss
When I ride her I feel the bliss
She is my little girl
I wouldn't swap her for the world.

She shakes her head like yes and no
She never ever steps on toes
Her colour changes every hour
She is almost like a springtime flower.

The first time I rode her
It was all just a blur
She tiptoed every step of the way
Like she knew it was my first day.

Shaye Little (12)
Whickham School, Whickham

Have You Seen The Soldiers?

Have you seen the soldiers out today?
Some are too young, some underpaid.
Why couldn't this country not just stay out of sight?
For some of these wars are not ours to fight.
When will this violence ever end?
Never?
Or just when there's no more soldiers to send.

Have you seen the soldiers out today?
Some are too young, some underpaid.
What kind of world do we live in?
A one of hate, war and sin?
Is war something that'll never cease?
Can we dispose of hate and introduce peace?
Is it really too much of a task?
To stay away from war, that's all we ask!

Have you seen the soldiers out today?

Thomas Fox (12)
Whickham School, Whickham

We Are The Geordie Boys

N ewcastle are my favourite team
E xcellent players
W inning is their dream
C arling Cup and FA Cup
A lways winning games
S coring goals and shiny players
T hey take their time to climb to the top
L osing players because of Mike Ashley
E vening games on Wednesday nights.

U nited stands hold, 52,000
N oloan is our Captain
I n the stadium it is always crowded
T heir nickname is the Geordie Boys
E very time they play it's always noisy
D ay after day the season ends.

Elliott Hancock (11)
Whickham School, Whickham

My Life

I could be out having fun like all the rest
How did life get like this, nothing to all day
Why did life get like this?

I'll tell you why,
I cracked under peer pressure, I took drugs
Drank far too much underage
Did stupid things, and every single one of them
Was to make me look cool.

But now I am the fool and the kids we thought were fools
Are the ones with everything we wanted
I've wasted my life away and I will *never* get it back.

So next time someone offers you some drugs walk away
Because trust me, you don't want to end up like me
Think you may feel like a fool but trust me,
You'll end up cool.

Hannah Hailes (12)
Whickham School, Whickham

My Cat

I have a cat
He is fat
He is black and white
He loves to fight
He is six
He does tricks
He likes me
He watches TV
He is my pet
He hates being wet
He likes drinks
He never thinks
He loves food
He is bad in a mood
He is a boy
He plays with his toy.

Daniel Thomas Adams (12)
Whickham School, Whickham

Hallowe'en Night

A ghost in the attic,
A black cat outside,
A wind and a whistle,
A scream to subside.

A ghoul in the garden,
An owl in the tree,
Its talons clinging tightly,
Its shadow clear to see.

The wail of a banshee,
A pumpkin glowing bright,
I'm going trick or treatin'
'Cause it's Hallowe'en tonight!

Anna Veitch (11)
Whickham School, Whickham

How The Other Half Live

Their reputation is bad
Their idea is mad
Making poor things fight
In the broad daylight.

Do we have no shame
For anyone else's pain?
Do we care
About what's out there?

Some people have no one
At least I have someone
Count yourself lucky
There's always someone worse off than you.

Charlotte Angus (12)
Whickham School, Whickham

Hallowe'en

On the night of Hallowe'en
Witches cackle and children are mean
Pumpkins glow in the soft candlelight
Lightning strikes and bats take flight

Lots of children eating sweets
At every house they shout, 'Trick or treat?'
Hidden behind their scary masks
Before rushing off to their next tasks.

As Hallowe'en night comes to a close
All evil spirits have to go
As the children follow in a dream
On the night of Hallowe'en.

Jack Hobson (11)
Whickham School, Whickham

Hallowe'en, Hallowe'en

Hallowe'en, Hallowe'en
What can you see?
Children dressing up,
Collecting sweets in a cup,
Trick or treat?
Choosing trick would be a cheat.

Children running through the night,
Dressing up scary, giving fright.
Giving out sweets on the porch,
When it's dark you'll need a torch.
Before the real witches come,
Get your sweets inside your tum.

Kara Michaela Lowes (12)
Whickham School, Whickham

Change

I have ears; you have ears
I have eyes; you have eyes
I have a nose; you have a nose
I have a mouth; you have a mouth
I have a family; you have a family
I have friends; you don't, so that's why you bully me.

I act polite; you act polite
My friends talk to me; you will make friends
I do well in class; you start to do well
I do homework; you do homework
Soon you'll have lots of friends and think
I've changed.

Ross Walker (14)
Whickham School, Whickham

I

I pretend to do something you actually do
I feel a feeling about something imaginary
I touch an imaginary touch
I worry about something that really bothers you
I cry about something that makes you very sad
I am something you actually pretend to be

I understand something you know is true
I say something you believe in
I dream something you actually dream about
I try something you really make an effort about
I hope something you actually hope for
I am something you know is true.

James Cooney
Whickham School, Whickham

- North Yorkshire & The North

Penny Wise Or Pound Foolish?

I was looking for a people carrier,
I found one advertised in Scotland with a broken timing belt,

So off I trekked on a Saturday morn,
With a trailer bouncing behind my beloved vehicle.

I bought the seven-seater for a knocked down price
Tracked home in a gale, trailer rocking and rolling,
Tried to repair on the cheap,
Never could put it right.

At the end of the day, it had to go to the professional

Was I penny wise or pound foolish?

Holly Robson (12)
Whickham School, Whickham

My Brother Matthew

I have a brother Matthew, he is really, really funny
But the only problem is he has bust his bones and lost all his money.
He is only 5 years old and he is a little monkey.
But lots of people think he is really chunky.
He has got me, my mum, my dad and my other brother too,
We've also got my other brother's girlfriend
And they love each other, *eww!*
I think it's really funny when we're hanging around together,
And we play this funny game called Little Miss Doctor Heather.

Megan Gates (11)
Whickham School, Whickham

I Will Never Forget Grandad

I'll never forget the times we had
I'll never forget whether good or bad
I'll never forget the laughter you brought
I'll never forget the things I've been taught.

I'll always remember when I'd sit on your knee.
I'll always remember the memories you shared with me.
I'll always remember when we'd walk a mile.
But most of all, I remember your smile.

Ellen Harrison (11)
Whickham School, Whickham

He's Not What You Think

He looks angry but he's not,
He looks like a murderer but he's not,
He looks rough but he's not,
He looks like a bad person but he's not,
He looks dangerous but he's not,
He looks like a hard man but he's not,
He looks vicious but he's not,
Don't judge a book by its cover.

Michael Pottinger (12)
Whickham School, Whickham

Labelled

Just because we have bottles doesn't mean it's drink
Just because we're hanging round doesn't mean we're up to something
Just because we cut across the grass doesn't mean we don't think
Just because we don't go to church doesn't mean we're full of sin
Just because some do drugs doesn't mean we all do
Just because a window smashed doesn't mean you look at me
Just because I'm a teenager doesn't mean I'm here to be blamed
It could be the old man next door so just let be!

Abbie Degnan (13)
Whickham School, Whickham

Yes We Are Teenagers

Yes we are rude,
Yes all of us do drugs,
Yes all of us are bad,
Yes all of us drink,
Yes all of us smoke,
Yes all of us are evil,
Yes we all seem bad,
But think, are we?

Robynne Clare (13)
Whickham School, Whickham

My Dad Is A Hero

My dad is a soldier.
I'm as proud as a peacock of him.
The gun he carries makes a din
But when he moves he's as silent as a pin.

When he comes home I am as happy as Larry
I can't wait for him to come home again
So that I can go to Spain.

Kane Harm (12)
Whickham School, Whickham

Autumn

The crisp autumn leaves fall to the ground,
Outside here there is no sound.
The raindrops beat upon the floor,
Outside in autumn is always a downpour
Days shortening,
Animals hibernating
What a beautiful time autumn is.

Corey Aitchison (11)
Whickham School, Whickham

Skating

S kater kids are the best
K J Johnson with the rest
A ll cool kids love to skate
T omorrow I might be out late
I ncluding fun, skating's great
N obody tells me what to do because
G oing skating's what I do.

Ben Gill (11)
Whickham School, Whickham

Lost

Like a blazing star,
Across the night sky,
Someone looking down on one,
Happy days have gone,
And sad days have come
And something has lost one
Something has to move on.

Sarah Bird (12)
Whickham School, Whickham

It's That Month Again

Hallowe'en is here and Bonfire Night.
Why is it always such a fright?

The weather is changing and the conkers are dropping,
All month long the birds are hopping!

The children are laughing and playing in the leaves.
It's that month again and a new season please!

Nicole Humphreys (11)
Whickham School, Whickham

BustARhyme - North Yorkshire & The North

Young Writers Information

We hope you have enjoyed reading this book - and that you will continue to enjoy it in the coming years.

If you like reading and writing poetry drop us a line, or give us a call, and we'll send you a free information pack.

Alternatively if you would like to order further copies of this book or any of our other titles, then please give us a call or log onto our website at www.youngwriters.co.uk

Young Writers Information
Remus House
Coltsfoot Drive
Peterborough
PE2 9JX
(01733) 890066